THE MEMOIRS OF AN EAST END PUBLICAN

To,

Tom & Bet.

Best wishes to you both.

God bless.

From your cousin,

Eddie Bagger.

THE MEMOIRS OF AN EAST END PUBLICAN

Eddie Cogger

Book Guild Publishing
Sussex, England

First published in Great Britain in 2010 by
The Book Guild Ltd
Pavilion View
19 New Road
Brighton, BN1 1UF

Typesetting in Garamond by
Keyboard Services, Luton, Bedfordshire

Printed and bound in Great Britain by
CPI Antony Rowe

A catalogue record for this book is available from
The British Library

ISBN 978 1 84624 509 1

Dedication

I would like to dedicate this book to my dearest Lena. I am deeply sorry for all the problems she had to put up with when, at my behest, we became publicans. She managed to do the job, whilst fighting with the demons in her head, although it was completely alien to her – always with her bubbly personality and a welcoming smile on her face.

I love her, and always will, until pop-off day comes along.

Back Row: Jean (sister-in-law), Alec (brother), me, Barry (brother), Lena, Pat (sister-in-law). Middle Row: My mum and dad. Front Row: Tina (sister).

Back Row: Darren (Barry's son), Tracey and Eddie (my sons). Front Row: Lorraine (Alec and Jean's daughter), my mum and dad and Julianne (Barry's daughter).

Me, my mum, and my dad and me (aged approx. 12) strolling along Ramsgate Promenade.

Family Tree

Great Grandparents

William Cogger Catherine Binfield

Grandparents

John Robert Cogger Edward H. Wadwell
Ada Edwards Annie Amelia Scarborough

Parents

Lawrence C. Cogger Florence Amelia Wadwell

Edward L. Cogger Alexander John Cogger
Barry Robin Cogger Catherine A. Cogger

Edward L. Cogger Lena I. Stovold

Edward Cogger Tracey Cogger

Edward Cogger Jennifer Day Tracey Cogger Tracey Lusher

Jade Cogger Amber Cogger
Gabrielle Cogger Ellis Cogger

Angeline Cogger Lennie Harris
Lennie J. Harris

Krystle Cogger James Hill
Bradley J. Hill

Contents

1	The River	1
2	The Build-up to the War	5
3	3rd September 1939	7
4	And So It Began	13
5	The Beauty of Wales	15
6	The War	17
7	The Blitz	19
8	Senior School	31
9	Leaving School	35
10	The Merchant Navy	41
11	Courtship	53
12	The Army Catering Corps	57
13	Promotion	69
14	The Wrong Man	71
15	Back to Barracks	75
16	Back to Camp	79
17	Last Leave Before Demob	81
18	Back to Camp for the Last Time	83
19	Cooking Tonight	85
20	A Cook's Revenge is Sweet	87

21	There's a Spy in My Soup	89
22	Back Home	91
23	Wedding Bells	93
24	The Wedding Party	97
25	Honeymoon in a 3-foot-wide Bed	101
26	Weekend Honeymoon Over	103
27	Mad House	111
28	Mad House (Part 2)	115
29	Two Tea Boys	119
30	Our New Home	121
31	A New Addition to the Family	127
32	A Stranger Appears	131
33	Return to Work	135
34	A New Beginning	141
35	A Change of Direction	145
36	The Thatched House, Barking	151
37	Back to the Thatched House	159
38	The *Sea Lena*	171
39	Back to the Boat	179
40	The Crown	185
41	Training Manager	193
42	The Beginning of the End	195
43	Prince Charlie	197
44	The Final Countdown	199
45	The Apartment in Cyprus	203
46	The End	209

Introduction

My name is Edward Lawrence Cogger and I am now 75 years old. I was born in Manor Park, an area in the East End of London in 1934 to Florence Amelia Cogger and Lawrence Charles Cogger. I have spent a year and a half putting my life down in print, to share my memories with my family and anyone who reads this book.

My granddad with my nan and my aunts Millie, Emm, Nell, Wynn, Lill, Lottie and Joan.

My nan and grandad Wadwell.

Acknowledgements

I would like to thank Sue Thomas and her partner Derek for their patience in trying to understand an amateur writing his life story.

Thank you too to my two sons, daughter-in-law, grandchildren and great-grandchildren for the love they give to me and little Lena.

I would also like to thank Arthur Gray and his daughter, Emma Brooks, for information gathered on my cousin, Arthur John Mann, who was killed on HMS *Hood*.

1

The River

When I was about four months old I moved with my mother and father to Dagenham, Essex (at the time the biggest council estate in Europe). My mother and father were both 20 years old when I was born. Little did they know of the journey through life they had set me upon. My upbringing was poor but happy and loving.

My father was a labourer who was working on the vast Becontree Estate which was being built at that time. My mother had been in domestic service before she had me. My paternal grandfather was born in December 1874, he was named John Robert, his father was William Cogger, my great grandfather. My great grandmother was Catherine Cogger, formerly Binfield. My grandmother was Ada Cogger (nee

Early photograph of my mum and dad.

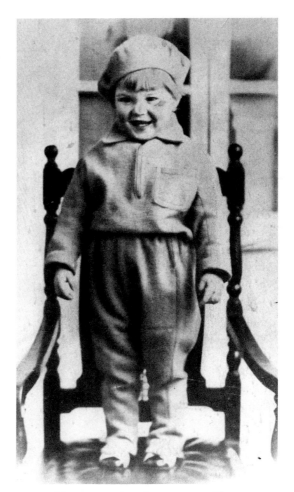

Me at approximately two years old.

Edwards). My maternal grandparents were Edward Henry Wadwell and Annie Amelia Wadwell (nee Scarborough).

I was told I was about two years of age when we (my mum, dad, uncle and aunt) had gone out for a day to Broxbourne by the river. I was playing with another child, a little girl a couple of years older than me. The girl was chasing me along the river bank when the bank collapsed, pitching me into the river.

To this day, approximately 70 years later, I can still remember what happened. I was aware of the bank crumbling and going under the water, aware of coming up and going down again, screaming for my parents, and then a moment of serene peacefulness.

I now know that my mum and dad couldn't swim and they were panicking and screaming on the bank of the river. People were jumping into the river but looking for me was futile. How long I lay on the river bed, I don't know, it seemed like ages. But suddenly I felt strong hands gradually pulling me to the surface. Being so young I wasn't aware of the person who saved me, but I am eternally grateful to him. As you will see later in the book, this wasn't the only time I had teetered on the edge of death.

Other early memories were around Christmas 1937. What I remember most about that Christmas was mum's stockings filled with oranges and apples, and the aromatic smell of tangerines. Nuts such as walnuts, brazils, cobs and chestnuts, being cooked on a shovel on a blazing fire. Those little Christmas paper chains that you link by licking the gummy ends to stick together. Little goodies included a little wooden train set, a teddy bear and other little odds and ends. I can recall my dad sliding me along the polished lino (no carpets in those days) and my dearest mum, who had a wonderful voice to match her beautiful face, hugging me tight and singing to me.

My early years are rather vague, although I do painfully remember sitting on a roadside kerb one day, sucking one of those big black lollypops (gobstoppers we called them in those days), when the largest bumble bee you could imagine (well, it was to me) landed on my lollypop and stung me on my lip. As you can imagine, I screamed my head off, very loudly!

For a time, when I was quite young, about three years old, I thought I lived in a circus, as our street was called Valence Circus. I had a little toy roundabout with tigers, lions, elephants, etcetera on it; maybe in my young mind I thought that that was the circus.

My father was a handsome young man. He had a nicely trimmed moustache and looked very much like the heart-throb film star of the day, Ronald Colman. He played the piano, not classical but he was a real old thumper of the keys. He also, like my mum, had a lovely voice. His favourite singer was Josef Locke, a famous tenor of the day. I loved to sit on his lap bouncing up and down as he stomped to the music of 'Hear My Song Violetta', his favourite tune.

I remember my mum and dad's photos on either side of the fireplace and I was intrigued by the way their eyes seemed to follow me around the room, as if they were keeping an eye on me.

In 1937 my mother gave birth to my brother; they named him Alexander. I have no memory of him being born, or much of him at all. Obviously I must have had my nose put out, but at three years of age it was probably also a novelty for me.

Life was wonderful then, the sun seemed to shine every day, butterflies were in abundance, one wouldn't see single butterflies, but hundreds. They would spiral upwards, twisting and turning, gently touching wings. Birds seemed to sing more, obviously because there were more of them then. Bumblebees and wasps buzzed merrily on their way, stopping frequently to collect pollen to fill the bulging sacs on their legs. Most of us had rabbits, cats and dogs as pets in those days; unfortunately the rabbits didn't last too long as the stew pot was their destiny!

I can't have known that my world would be full of cruelty, fear and terror.

2

The Build-up to the War

Obviously I had no recollection or knowledge of the impending war or the build-up to it. One could feel a strange sense of unease at home and in the community at large, and even at my young age I could feel that something was wrong. My mum and dad seemed subdued and spoke quietly when I was around them; I was soon to find out why.

I started infants' school at the beginning of 1939 when I was just five years old. I cannot remember much of those early schooldays, but some lingering memories do come back. For example, the little stubby milk bottles with a cardboard top and with a hole to push a straw into, mid-morning lie-downs on raffia mats, wearing little smocks to avoid getting covered in paint.

Sometime at the beginning of 1939 we were to experience a new contraption which was quite frightening: the gas mask. It was very claustrophobic, so the authorities, being aware that this would be a concern to young children, tried to make them less frightening by making them into fun caricatures – I remember mine was Mickey Mouse. From then on we had to take the mask in its little cardboard box everywhere we went.

My baby brother had an even worse situation: he had a full body contraption. He would be placed in the mask which would be zipped up, but you would be able to see his face through a little plastic window. It had a pump which had a filter attached and my mum or dad would use this to pump air into the little capsule.

At about the same time, there was much activity going on in the back gardens; we found out that every house was going to have its own air raid shelter. And so the shelters arrived: these were erected in oval-shaped corrugated iron partitions something like an oil drum cut in half, which made up the sides and the roof. A pit was dug in the ground in which four wooden bunks were built. A small wall was erected at the entrance and the whole contraption was covered in the earth which was taken out of the pit earlier, and then the whole thing was reinforced with sandbags.

In those days, due to the shortage of food, we all had ration books that meant when our mothers went shopping they handed over the family's ration book. People queued for many hours, sometimes without being able to get any food as the shop had run out of stock. The portions we were allowed were unbelievably small, ounces being the norm for each individual.

Parents, especially the mothers, devised many ingenious methods to beat the system. One of the favourite ways of doing this was by sending the kids to the shops to get the shopping, but the kids were unaware that the mothers had craftily removed the stamp mark put on by the grocer, simply by rubbing it out with a piece of bread. Many a shop assistant was berated by an angry mother for accusing her of such practices, protesting her innocence, and that she would never use her child for such a deed. Many mothers had to resort to these desperate measures to feed their children.

Well … going back to the gardens. In those days there used to be a slogan on all the billboards which read 'Dig for Victory', so that any piece of available land was dug over and allotments began springing up in the most unusual places, eventually even on bomb sites. Unfortunately the shelter had taken away a lot of our garden which our dad used as an allotment, so this meant our food source was greatly diminished.

It was late in the summer of 1939 (I was only five years old by then), and still I remember two new words being spoken by our parents: 'war' and 'evacuation'. Although it meant nothing to me then, my young life would be changed forever. This situation was totally new to us children: we would apparently be going to safer places around Britain.

3

3rd September 1939

The day war was declared, I can remember to this day, 70 years on. As you would expect, Britain had been preparing for this war, and not being a war historian, just a five-year-old boy at the time, I can only comment on my own experiences.

I remember I had only just started school, and because the corridors were being made bomb blast-proof we were sent in small groups to various homes in the locality to continue our schooling. A few months before the start of the war, there were many routines we had to perform. We had months of air raid practices, and the sirens wailed so loudly that they sent fear to the pit of your stomach. Air raid wardens were now beginning to become more noticeable. These were elderly men who made their presence known by shouting out very loudly, 'Put that light out' – at night of course!

I suppose the inevitable was bound to happen but it came so suddenly – an air raid. I was playing about 30 yards from my house when suddenly a low, eerie whine began. It built up into a terrifying crescendo. The young ones amongst us were screaming and panicking, not knowing which way to turn. Wardens were blowing their whistles, arms waving this way and that, no one had a clue what was happening. Utter chaos. I heard a shout and turned to see my father running to me; he gathered me up into his arms and ran like the wind to the safety of the shelter. We later learned that it had been a false alarm. It was mistakenly thought to have been a German fighter plane. My dad was not called up as he was in construction and was a steel erecter working on aircraft hangers.

When Neville Chamberlain announced we were now at war with Germany, it didn't make much difference to us younger ones. We were not aware of what was to come. It was quite difficult for me to understand at that time just what was going on.

Finally we found out. Our parents had been summoned to the school to discuss the organisation of an evacuation. My parents had decided that I should go, along with the majority of the pupils at the school. Many of the mothers decided to evacuate with their children. Unfortunately for me my mother, having a very young baby, couldn't go with me.

It didn't take long to organise and the day came when we were all assembled at the school gates. The coaches, which were to take us to the railway station, were already waiting for us. I asked my mum where we were going and with tears streaming down her beautiful face she replied, 'To Wales'. With tears now overwhelming me, I got on the coach and with the window separating us we both broke down. The engine of the coach started up and when I next looked up my darling mum had gone.

I must have cried for most of the journey, as did most of the younger ones, but we eventually arrived at the railway station which I have since learned was Paddington. And so began my journey to the land of chapels and hell. The Welsh people had volunteered to take in young people who were considered at risk in London and the South Eastern areas.

The journey to Wales seemed to take forever; we were so bored as we had nothing to amuse ourselves with. I spent most of my time looking out of the open window, breathing in that unforgettable smell of the train engine smoke, the odd speck of cinder hitting my face.

Eventually the train began to reduce speed and it appeared that we were approaching our destination. As the train began to slowly reach the platform, the elder children read out the signboards, which said 'Blaina'. My nightmare was about to begin.

When we stepped off of the train we looked around us in amazement, for the track and station were situated in between two enormous mountains; it was an unbelievable sight.

As we were getting organised by the various welfare people we realised we couldn't understand them; well, not properly. They seemed to sing their words: low one moment, high the next, anyway it was extremely difficult for a five-year-old Cockney kid like me. We were all lined up in rows of about a dozen kids to each row.

Eventually we were all led off in different directions; my group was taken to the right of the station which had back gardens leading to the railway lines. The welfare lady waddled along in front of us, like a mother duck with her brood of ducklings following in her wake. As we reached the neat row of terraced houses the householders were standing around in little groups, inquisitively looking and wondering who they would be getting. Gradually my little troop diminished and then it was my turn.

'Hello Mrs Jones,' said Mother Duck. 'I have your evacuee here. His name is Edward.'

Mrs Jones looked at me and almost spat out her words. 'Him? Him? I wanted someone bigger to look after my Tommy,' she said, ushering a figure from behind her.

What appeared was a hulking figure of a boy of about nine years old, about 12 inches taller than me and 5 stone heavier. My heart sank.

Mrs Jones ushered me in. She obviously had not been expecting a shrimp like me and she made it plain by her actions. 'I don't know what your father will say when he gets home from the mine, he won't be too pleased to see him,' she said, indicating me with her head.

'I guess not, Mum,' Tommy replied, with a glimmer in his eyes that sent a shiver down my spine.

As I stepped into the neat front room of the house my eyes swept swiftly around, taking note of what was to be home for the ensuing 12 months or so. The first thing I saw was a roaring fire, and alongside it was one of those beautiful dressers which seemed to be traditional in the valleys of Wales. It must have been Mrs Jones's pride and joy, saucers and plates all lovingly positioned, with all the china cups on hooks, gently rocking to any movement that was being created in the room, especially when a train lumbered by. Looking further around the room I saw a door which led to the pantry, and another door to the coal cellar, which was ultimately to be (as a very frightened five-year-old), a torture chamber.

After the formalities were seen to, I was introduced to Tommy. He looked even bigger than my first impression of him, and next to me he was gigantic. Later in the day, after some tea and biscuits, I was shown the bedroom I would be sharing with Tom. In the room was a double bed, which I was accustomed to at home, sharing with my younger brother.

As the front door led directly into the front room, I was surprised when it suddenly opened, and in walked a man, his face as black as ink (I was later to find out this was coal dust), the whites of his eyes standing out frighteningly. As he looked around the room he caught sight of me, cowering on a chair.

'Is this him, then?' he asked. 'Bit of a squirt, isn't he?' he said, in his lilting melodic accent.

'Yes, she said that most of them were small,' said Mrs Jones, referring to Mother Duck. 'Come on then, you two,' said Mrs Jones. 'Bath and bed. I suppose you're very tired after that long journey you had today.'

I nodded my head in agreement. I was most surprised when Mrs Jones went to the coal cupboard, and with much banging and clanging pulled out a tin bath. I was aware that I hadn't been to the toilet for quite a while now and asked Mrs Jones where the bathroom was, she looked at me in amazement and without a word told Tom to take me to the toilet which I was to find out was in the back yard. It reminded me very much of my granny's house in east London.

Tom and I hadn't spoken to each other much yet so I asked him, 'Where do you have a bath, Tom?'

He replied, 'In front of the fire, we have the clothes horse in front of us.'

This is going to be different I thought to myself, thinking of the new council house, with the lovely big bathroom at home.

The procedure for having a bath was of a primitive nature; firstly a large pot of cold water was put on an enormous black stove, which had six different-sized round holes on top and an equivalent amount of tops to fit the holes. In the front of the stove was a large oven; by the side of the oven was a door where the coal was shovelled in. When the pot had eventually boiled it was poured into the tin bath, cold water was added to get the right temperature and the procedure was repeated again for the next one.

Tom was the first one to have his bath, the clothes horse already put in place by his mum. Then came my turn. Unfortunately I had to use the same water as he had. To make matters even more amazing, after renewing the water Mr Jones (black as the ace of spades, due to the coal dust that he was covered in) stepped behind the clothes horse and proceeded to have his bath.

Eventually it was time to get prepared for bed, and having asked Mrs Jones to use the toilet, she gave me a torch and I went out into the dark. When I returned (you must remember that I am relating this in the language and mind of a five-year-old), I saw no sign of young Tom. There wasn't, as far as I could see, anyone in the room. I called out and heard a noise behind the clothes horse. Looking over I was shocked at what I saw: Tom was doing a poo on a pile of newspapers (because he was frightened to go outside in the dark). He started screaming at me, which resulted in his parents rushing into the room.

'He was looking at me,' he said over and over again.

His father's eyes glaring at me, he said, 'If you ever do that again it will be my belt on your arse and the night in the coal cellar.'

Looking at Tom, I again saw that look of evil I had seen earlier in the day. I didn't know then that I would be spending many nights with a sore bum in that cellar. That night I cried myself to sleep. 'Where are you, Mummy,' I cried. 'Where are you?'

4

And So It Began

It was obvious that I would face further threats from Tom. He had seen the reaction from his father towards me the previous night and he would take advantage of that. Tom was a bully of the worst kind, a spoilt cry-baby, a coward and, unfortunately for me, he had parents who encouraged him. I was half his size and weight and a very unhappy little boy.

The first time I experienced physical abuse was when we were playing on the bed, bouncing on it like a trampoline. Unfortunately Tom bounced off the bed. I don't know if he hurt himself but he certainly screamed his head off.

His mother came rushing up the stairs, her face all red and flustered exclaiming, 'What on earth is going on?'

'It was him, Mummy,' he replied, pointing at me. 'He pushed me off the bed.' Crocodile tears began to run down his face.

I tried to explain that we were playing, but she wouldn't listen. 'Just you wait till Mr Jones gets home from work, my boy; he will soon sort you out no tea for you tonight,' she said.

I dreaded his coming home, especially after my previous experience with him. Eventually I heard the key turn in the lock and in walked Mr Jones.

Looking around the room he said, 'You two are quiet.'

The whites of his eyes were piercing in the coal black of his face. Mrs Jones beckoned Mr Jones over to her and a whispered conversation took place between them.

He returned to me, grabbed me by the scruff of my neck and said, 'Like to play rough, do you? Well let's see how a couple of hours in the dark suit you.' With that he opened the coal cupboard door and threw me in.

I was screaming with fear. 'Please let me out!' I cried, but to no avail.

I eventually fell asleep after sobbing my heart out. The door was finally opened, and as I looked around me I was amazed to see lots of empty cigarette packets strewn all over the cellar, Tom Jones Senior was a chain smoker. As I left the cellar I happened to look into a mirror; my face was as black as Mr Jones's had been, but stained with tears.

I had been introduced to the cellar. It would be the first of many nights I would spend there. Later in my life I would suffer from claustrophobia, which I attributed to my nights in the cellar.

5

The Beauty of Wales

The bullying by young Tom and the abuse I suffered from his father was ongoing, but despite all that, I still love Wales today, for its scenery. In fact, about 30 years ago (I was in my early forties then), my wife, my two teenage sons and I went to a tiny village called Mousehole where we had been going for many years for a holiday.

In all the years we had been going to Cornwall I hadn't given it a thought that Wales was on the other side of the Severn Bridge. One day as we were travelling, on the spur of the moment I followed the road which was signposted to Wales. We drove to the other side of the

Lena, Tracey and Eddie in Mousehole, Cornwall.

bridge and I then began to have doubts. I didn't know where Blaina was or how I could find it. Eventually we came to an inn; I went in and asked if he could direct me to Blaina. Well, what with his Welsh accent and my East End Cockney talk it was a wonder we got anywhere at all, but in the end we ended up having a good laugh with each other. I told him about being a wartime evacuee in Wales but didn't give any details of my experiences.

The journey onwards was of unbelievable beauty; mountains soaring hundreds of feet both sides of us – it was a scenic wonderland. As we travelled further into the valley I began to realise where we were: there was the railway in between two mountains, leading to a railway station, Blaina. I had arrived back to face the demons of the early years of my life.

We parked the car on a garage forecourt (which hadn't been there in my time) and I just soaked up the beauty of it all, even though I had suffered such abuse as a child. As the mining village only had one road, identifying the house I had stayed in was quite easy. Also, it was etched in my memory, even after all these years.

I determinedly strode up to the front door, lifted my arm to reach the door knocker and hesitated; doubts began to surge in my brain. I hadn't thought this out; they would be in their eighties by now, probably dead, and Tom would be older than me. I took a step or two backwards, thought about it, and turned back to the car. I drove back to the Severn Bridge and never went back to Wales again.

6

The War

My mother, due to her commitment to her new baby and my father now working away from home, was only able to visit me once in the first year with the Joneses. She found her little son, who she thought she was sending to a place of refuge, now an introverted, frightened, fearful wreck of a child. My mother, who had a fearsome temper, demanded to know what had happened to me.

Mrs Jones blustered an explanation that she hadn't expected such a young child and that she couldn't cope with me. My mother questioned me as to what had happened, but I was too frightened to tell her, fearing that I would have to face the music when she left. My fears were unfounded when she told me she was taking me home that day, which she did, giving Mrs Jones a good old Cockney clout as we left.

The war had been ongoing for about a year when I returned, and things had changed greatly in that time. The Home Guard had been formed (Dads' Army). Wardens now patrolled the streets and all the shelters had been completed, with all the schools having their corridors blast-proofed. Artillery guns had been situated in local parks, hidden under huge sheets of camouflage. Barrage balloons were also placed in the parks to protect the gun emplacements.

I was now attending Charlicote Junior School, Dagenham Essex, just fifty yards from where I lived in Valence Circus, Dagenham. For the young ones who didn't realise the danger which was soon to come, we couldn't contain the excitement of it all.

I missed my dad a great deal at this time. As I explained earlier, he wasn't called up for the services as he was in construction (building aircraft hangers) and this was classed as vital to the war effort, but he was often away for months at a time. My mum, along with other women, was sent to various factories in the Dagenham area. She was sent to Briggs Motor Company, which made car bodies and jerry cans (petrol containers) etcetera. Briggs was a subsidiary of the Ford Motor Company, later taken over by them.

On 7th September 1940 the Blitz started. My recollection of that first day was of the sirens, which began with a slow, eerie wail, building up to an unbelievable ear-splitting crescendo, then slowly dying away again. The air raid wardens quickly took control, gas masks at the ready, rattles in case of a gas attack at hand, ordering us quickly to our shelters. My mum got us organised in the shelter, making sure we were as far back as we could get.

This being my first air raid since coming back from Wales I was eager to see as much as I could. So I began to edge myself closer to the opening of the shelter, gradually poking my head out. I could hear the guns in the parks beginning to open fire and see the barrage balloons starting to rise.

Suddenly I heard the drone of an airplane in the distance. I heard the stuttering of machine gun fire and then a terrific explosion. Looking out quickly, I saw that a barrage balloon had been hit and had exploded, and a fighter plane was strafing the vicinity. My mother was screaming at me to get my head back into the shelter, which I did rapidly.

After a while the 'all clear' siren sounded and we climbed out of the shelter and looked around to see what damage had been caused. We found out that little harm had been done, just some bullet holes here and there, although the gun emplacements had some injured soldiers. It was said that the plane was on a reconnaissance flight. The conversation amongst the locals was all of the morning's attack. The majority were very frightened, especially those whose husbands were away in the Army.

7

The Blitz

We lived about 2 miles from the River Thames and that, unfortunately, turned out to be a very dangerous place to live. Apparently the German aircraft that had attacked us in the morning was on a mission to test out the defences on the way to London by following the course of the Thames.

That night towards dusk, we all (my mum, my young brother and I) went to bed, my mum in her room my brother and I in ours. Suddenly we were awakened by the wailing of the siren. It sent a terrible shiver down my spine and into my heart. I heard dull thuds in the distance the like of which I had never heard before.

Jumping out of bed, I looked out of my bedroom window and what I saw was an almost unbelievable sight. There were many, maybe 100 or so, German bombers with their fighter escorts flying up the Thames towards London. Many were trapped in the glare of the searchlights which criss-crossed the night sky. Many of the planes were shot down but many got through and caused a terrible amount of death and damage that night.

Meanwhile whilst all this was going on, my mother was desperately screaming for me to get to the shelter. During all the excitement I had become completely absorbed in watching this spectacle, although I was terribly mortified at the death toll when I found out.

We had to suffer many, many months of this constant bombardment; it seemed to be never-ending. We lost many young school friends in those days; we were told many times at assembly of the death or injuries to our classmates.

We saw very little of our dad during the early days of the war, only a short visit every now and then but we had a lovely surprise when mum told my brother and I that she was expecting another baby. As my mum got nearer to her time, she asked her mother and father if they would come and look after us for her whilst she had her baby, which they agreed to.

I loved my granddad; he was a perfect gentleman, smart, upright with a really bushy moustache. The story goes that he was shot over a cockfight feud and was taken to hospital on a wheelbarrow where he had a lung removed. My gran on the other hand was a real terror, only 4 feet 2 in her crinkly-stockinged feet she was a real handful with her fiery temper; no wonder my mum was a spitfire too. On 16th June 1941 my mum had her baby, another boy, calling him Barry Robin.

As the war progressed we had many frightening experiences. We were being bombed day and night now, and hardly left the shelter. This made it particularly difficult for my mum, especially with my two young siblings to contend with. She couldn't cope with the things she would be expected to do so a lot was put on my shoulders, mainly caring for my three-year-old brother. Although things were pretty tough at that time we still managed to amuse ourselves in different ways, one being to copy the goose-stepping style of the Nazi Army. We had great fun in taking the mickey out of Adolf Hitler by sticking two fingers under our noses (to replicate his moustache) and goose-stepping with a bent-arm salute like he did.

We had to contend with many other dangers. With the continuous day and night bombings, we were also now experiencing parachute time bombs which floated down, exploding many hours later after the 'all clear' sirens had sounded.

My paternal grandparents also had some terrible news delivered to them. Their grandson had been reported killed on the battleship

In Remembrance of
ARTHUR JOHN MANN

Service: Royal Navy

Rating: Ordinary Seaman

Serial Number: P/JX 220863

Date Joined *Hood*: Unknown

Biographical Information: Arthur was the son of Mr and Mrs Benjamin Mann, of Ilford, Essex. He was 20 years old at the time of his loss. We have no additional information.

In Remembrance of
THOMAS EDWARD COGGER

Service: Royal Marines

Rank: Marine

Service Number: PO/21115

Date Joined *Hood*: February 1940

Biographical Information: Thomas was the husband of Kathleen Cogger, of Fareham, Hampshire. He was the son of William and Eliza Cogger. Thomas was a member of 'X' turrets gun crew. Prior to serving in Hood, Thomas spent seven years aboard the Royal Yacht, 'Victoria and Albert'. He was 39 years old at the time of his loss. We have no additional information.

John Robert Cogger,
killed at sea during the war.

HMS *Hood*. The war had now affected my family. He was my cousin, my aunt Milly's son, Arthur John Mann. My grandmother on my father's side had 15 children, losing four in childbirth. One little boy, Georgie, died climbing a lamppost – he twisted his gut; one died of diphtheria. My dad was now the last son to survive.

There is also an extraordinary coincidence that two relations might have served on HMS *Hood* at the time of my aunt's loss. Whilst searching for information for this book, I received from one of my cousins a photo showing that there was a Thomas Edward Cogger on the *Hood*. Could this be just a coincidence? The name Cogger is a pretty unusual surname but I also received from my cousin the information commemorating a 'Thomas Edward Cogger', lost in the sinking of HMS *Hood*, 'brother of Miss Ada Cogger' – my grandmother's name. Coincidence?

The sea and rivers have seemingly had a great effect on my families' fortunes. Apart from my river experiences before and after that time, I also have a cousin named Pearl Woolf who was one of only 25 to survive the sinking of HMS *Wakeful*. This ship was laden with troops picked up near Dunkirk and was blown apart whilst heading for Britain.

Later that year we received a greater shock that would affect our immediate family. My dad had fallen 60 feet and was gravely ill. He had suffered many injuries including broken legs, skull and jaw, and cuts that required many stitches, and he was not expected to survive, such were his injuries. My mum was immediately rushed, by his employers, to the hospital in Bury St Edmunds where my dad was being treated.

HMS WAKEFUL		
■ Class: Admiralty V & W ■ Pennant: H88 ■ Built by: John Brown Shipbuilding & Engineering	Company Ltd (Clydebank, Scotland) ■ Laid down: January 17, 1917	■ Launched: October 6, 1917 ■ Commissioned: November 16, 1917 ■ Lost: May 29, 1940

HMS *Wakeful*

My aunt Rose and uncle Lenn, cousin Lennie, me and cousins Cathy and Ronnie.

My mum's sister came to take us to where she lived in Hornchurch, where we stayed for approximately four weeks. We had a lovely time; there were many farm animals which we rarely saw in Dagenham. I loved it in Hornchurch, especially with my three cousins, it was in the summer and, as the saying goes, it was always sunny in those days. There was just a little problem we had to worry about. Although Hornchurch was a rural area in those days, it had just one drawback: a blooming great Spitfire aerodrome base there. This was the main base in the South East of England for the defence of London.

My mum eventually came home but she was very worried about my dad's condition. She said he would probably be in hospital for at least a year. I then realised I would have to act in his place as the man of the house.

London was taking a really terrible pounding night after night, with no respite. We lived about 7 miles from the East End of London and we could hear the massive explosions as the bombs were hitting their targets. There was a constant glow in the sky as it was lit up by the enormous fires that swept the horizon.

The actual Blitz of London lasted about nine months, the loss of life and devastation to the city was unbelievable. Hardly a building was left standing, and the rest had serious damage, but the courage of the Londoners had held fast. The courage and bravery shown by the firemen, ambulance crews, police, Home Guard, WVS, and many of the other volunteer services was a true reflection of the spirit of the Londoners. King George and Queen Elizabeth were regularly to be seen inspecting bomb sites, lifting the spirits of the nation.

The Germans had lost so many planes and pilots that they directed their efforts to other areas – unfortunately for us as the brunt of the bombing had now turned to the suburbs. Night after night we took to the shelter and basically stayed there for nights on end. The days were not as bad as the nights; our mothers could hurriedly nip out to the shops to get some shopping. Unfortunately I was the babysitter on those occasions.

One night, just as the sirens had started sounding, almost immediately there was a tremendous explosion close by which prevented us from getting to the shelter. We were trapped in the house. Suddenly there was a brilliant white glare which appeared to engulf the whole of the back garden area. My mum, although frightened as hell, tried her hardest not to show her fear to us but I could see she was beginning to panic.

We began to bang on the wall that separated the next door neighbours' house from ours, calling out their names: 'Mr Spooner. Can you help us?' This had no effect so Mum decided to go to the front door, as the flames did not appear to be so intense there as they were at the back of the house.

When she was able to get the front door open, which had been blown off its hinges, we found that the entire street had been hit by a load of incendiary bombs (phosphorous), hence the intense white glare. These bombs are carried by the bomber plane in what was called a 'bread basket'. The basket opened when the plane was very high and spread the bombs over a very wide area, basically causing a firestorm, havoc and death.

When the morning arrived, the destruction we observed was indescribable. Many houses had been totally destroyed; others, once happy loving homes, now reduced to rubble. Death and terrible injuries had rained down on us and I shall never forget that night.

We were very lucky to get away with minor blast damage to our house that night, but the next day was just as deadly for us kids, due to unexploded incendiary bombs. As I explained earlier, incendiary bombs are carried in an aircraft in contraptions we knew as a breadbasket. These are loaded with hundreds of bombs and when the bomb bay is opened the basket drops about a thousand feet and then opens up allowing it to deliver its deadly cargo. However many of these bombs did not detonate, so the warden's job was to carefully dig around the bomb and then disarm them. They were often easy to find as the fin used to protrude out of the ground.

As you may be able to imagine (or can you?), we became wardens' assistants (obviously without their knowledge) and with garden forks, shovels and anything that came to hand, we began to prise the bomb out of the ground. It didn't take long for the wardens to cotton on to us and of course, we got a 'walloping' from mum.

Amongst all this mayhem and carnage there was some laughter. One such incident I can recall relates to Mr Spooner and his sons. When the 'all clear' warning had sounded all the elder men and young men began to help the firemen and wardens to fight the fires, and Mr Spooner and his sons joined in enthusiastically. Unfortunately for them, in the excitement of the moment they were not aware that the bread basket had fallen into Mr Spooner's prize pear tree, which was blazing away. It was just one moment of light-heartedness amongst the carnage of which there was plenty more to come.

It's hard to imagine now, but I can remember the breadman, the milkman, the street singer, the horse-drawn childrens' roundabout, the ragman who gave a goldfish in a bowl for a bundle of old clothes, and the knife sharpener. He used to pedal his bike as fast as his legs would go to drive his grinder (I can't remember now how his bike never moved, but it was static as he pedalled). I remember getting a job with our milkman, George, when I was about eight years old. I had to get up at 6 a.m. and be at the milk yard at 6.30 a.m. I then loaded up the crates whilst George saddled up Daisy the horse.

Daisy unfortunately was blind, but she seemed to have a sixth sense. She would walk on for about 10 yards then stop whilst we delivered the milk, then go on again. However, one day the sirens went off, she bolted, broke a leg and had to be put down. I was heartbroken for weeks, as it felt that as I looked into her sightless eyes she was begging me to help her. I am afraid the gun was the only relief from her suffering.

I always hoped that one day I would own my own business, so my next venture was as a paper boy. Many boys of my age sold papers on street corners. I was still only about eight years old but I stood on my corner: 'Paper, Paper, *Daily Herald, Star, Evening News*', I would cry out. I gave my mum most of my earnings as my dad was still very ill and my mum was still struggling, money-wise.

We had some better news relating to my dad as he was showing physical improvement, although suffering from depression due to not being able to see his wife and children. He could come home if it was possible for him to continue his nursing at home. My mum was asked if she could manage him at home if she was given certain home assistance, which she readily agreed to.

Before my dad came home a new type of shelter was installed in the

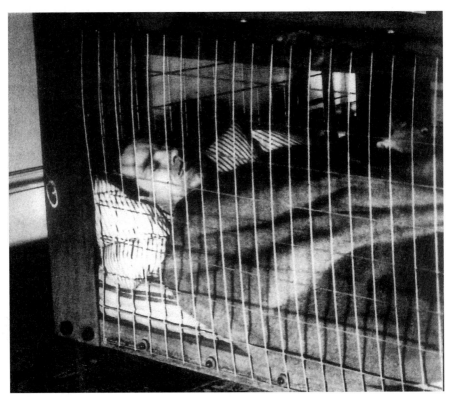

I don't know if this is my dad in a Morrison Shelter but it looks very much like him.

front room. It was called a Morrison Shelter and was for people who were severely disabled. It was like a strong cage made of steel with a metal mesh around the sides, about 4 feet wide by 6 feet long. We couldn't wait for the day to come when our dad would be coming home. We were so excited, especially my two younger siblings who hadn't seen much of him at all, particularly the baby Barry.

The day finally arrived when a big Army ambulance pulled up outside our house. It was so exciting. All the neighbours were outside our house as my dad was carried into our house on a stretcher. I was so proud of him, having fallen 60 feet and lived to tell the tale.

When he had been settled in his 'cage' (as we called it), the full extent of his injuries could be seen. Even though his fall had been at least eight months previously, his body was still badly broken. He had a plaster cast from just below his neck going all the way down to his left ankle. He had suffered many serious injuries and would take many, many years to recover, and he would be left with a severe limp for the rest of his life as his left leg was now 2 inches shorter than the right.

In the months to come my father remained bedridden so we had the opportunity to go into the cage with him. Despite all the bombings and all the dangers we faced, we stayed in the cage with him and my mum and all five of us cuddled each other until we fell asleep. The scent that came from him was as I had always remembered, the odour of my dad. God bless him.

The bombing carried on relentlessly but my dad improved somewhat. He had his plaster removed and leg irons fitted; even so he was still dependent on the cage, but was relieved to be more mobile as he was now on crutches.

The war had been going for about four years now and the Germans had advanced to most of the continent of Europe, setting up concentration camps as they went, killing millions of men, women and children by the cruellest methods imaginable. The air raids were still not letting up and we were not getting much respite day or night.

One day there was a lull in the bombing so it gave us a chance to play. One of our games was to play with an old bicycle wheel with no tyres on and a short stick to propel it with. Unfortunately my wheel was somewhat buckled and wobbled about a bit, causing me to run into it. The wheel was a rusty old one I had found on a bomb site, with the consequence being that I was sent to the local hospital where a 6-inch gash was clipped together – no stitches in those days!

My dad had now discarded one of his leg irons so it gave us another thing to play with, especially me, with my leg all bandaged up. My leg was about a foot shorter than the iron but we still had great fun with it, Long John Silver had nothing on me!

However the war was still with us and a new threat was about to descend upon us. It had various names: the Doodle Bug, the Flying Bomb, the Buzz Bomb and the V1. It was launched from France as it was like a plane, with an engine attached to the rear of it, and had just enough fuel to reach the South East of England. The engine would cut out when the fuel was spent and the plane would glide silently, gradually losing height until hitting indiscriminately, detonating its lethal contents on the innocent unsuspecting citizens below.

One day my brothers and I were playing in our local park and decided that we would go scrumping from an orchard that had an iron railing fence around it. It was a favourite place for scrumpers but the fence was about 5 feet high and had spikes on top. I knew from previous experience that there were gaps in the fence where other scrumpers had forced the bars apart. Due to my leg injury I wouldn't be able to climb the trees, so I told my middle brother to squeeze through the bars. My mum had bought him a brand new pair of shoes that morning and he found he had difficulty climbing the trees as his shoes were too slippery, so I told him to take his shoes off, which he did.

He was merrily picking the apples and putting them inside his shirt when the siren went. I shouted to my brother to come quickly and as we were running away from the park we heard this most terrifying sound which is almost too horrifying to describe. The deep stuttering roar was deafening, and looking behind us I could see it was about 100 yards behind us, about 50 feet above our heads and coming straight at us. The stuttering of the engine was a sign that the flying bomb had run out of fuel. As we ran out of the park gates it flew about 40 feet above our heads aiming straight for our house, disappeared over our house, and seconds later the enormous explosion blew us off our feet.

We picked ourselves up and ran hell for leather to our home which I was certain had been hit as a large plume of flames and smoke began to rise from the area where we lived. We only lived about 200 yards from the park entrance and I feared the worst as we turned into our road. The reliving of that experience has always haunted me, even to this day.

Our house was intact. The bomb had actually flown just above the rooftops and came down in the next road, but it caused death, injuries and destruction. It was said that a Canadian soldier waiting in a bus queue was decapitated. Others were killed: many people who I knew, schoolmates included.

My dad was terribly worried about our well-being. He was in his shelter, having had no information about us, or of our mum, who was now back at work. To make matters worse, whilst we were running home I noticed that my leg was bleeding profusely as the clips had parted from the flesh, and then I noticed my brother was barefooted. We had forgotten his new shoes lying at the base of the tree. Boy, was I in trouble. All our lying didn't convince Mum, who really laid into us. I then had to go through all the pain of having the clips reinserted again.

The last person injured in our house at the end of the war was my younger brother Barry. There was a lot of ammunition being brought back from the war by the soldiers, and we had somehow obtained some bullets. A group of about five of us tried to find a way of getting one of the bullets to explode. First we tried hitting it with a hammer with no success, so after many suggestions we decided to light a fire and throw a bullet into the fire. Nothing happened. We then stirred the fire up and my little brother bent over it and blew onto the flames to get the centre of the fire as hot as was possible. Suddenly there was a terrific, deafening bang. We all fell backwards at this sudden explosion, our ears ringing, all of us in a state of shock. But worst of all, my little brother was bleeding heavily from a wound to his chin. I don't know if the bullet or some fragments of the casing had grazed his chin, but how could I expect my mother and father to believe that he had been hurt by a live bullet? When I was asked how he had hurt himself, I lied and said he had fallen over. Wouldn't you? Who would have believed me?

The flying bomb era lasted about a year. However, Hitler had another terrible weapon to inflict more terror upon us, the V2 rockets. These were the most fearsome weapons of all to the population as there was no warning at all; they just fell indiscriminately out of the sky.

The Germans were now really taking a beating after the brilliant evacuation from Dunkirk; the Allies were gathering their armies to invade France. The Russians were now on the offensive in the East, so there was a feeling of hope within the population now. This was finally the beginning of the end for the mighty German war machine. The Allies had retreated back to the UK by any means possible. More than 50,000 British and American troops came back to the UK in any craft that sailed, including war ships, cargo ships, pleasure boats, trawlers, dinghies and anything else that floated! It was the most successful evacuation of all time and when they had regrouped, the Allies began the fight back, starting with the invasion of Normandy in France and steadily into Europe until they had joined up with the Russians.

When he realised he could not win the war, Hitler along with his mistress Eva Braun, some of his henchmen and their families, all retreated to a specially prepared underground bunker in the centre of Berlin. The Allies were still finding themselves up against strong resistance and the war carried on for a few more months. We were to learn that Hitler, Eva Braun and his faithful generals and their families had all committed suicide. The only one left alive at that time was Hitler's manservant. Hitler had given him instructions to take his and Eva's bodies outside the bunker and burn them. He then killed himself. The bodies were later confirmed as Hitler and Braun.

After the war the Nuremberg Trials began. The accused were responsible for the deaths of millions of Jews in the concentration camps. The rest of the German hierarchy were tried and either sentenced to death or sent to prison for many years.

On VE Day (Victory in Europe), many street parties were held up and down the country. I can remember it as if it were yesterday. I recall charging about with an enormous Union Jack held high and yelling as loud as I could, 'We won the war, we won the war!' We were all so excited.

Japan soon followed (VJ Day). The Americans had suffered enormous losses in the Far East, as had the British. As the Japanese refused to surrender, two atomic bombs were dropped on them resulting in many hundreds of thousands of deaths and injuries. Although the Japanese had committed many terrible atrocities against the Americans and British, one couldn't help feeling very sad for them.

8

Senior School

When I reached the age of eleven, having failed the exam to go to high school, I was sent to the local secondary school, Halbutt Road Senior School for Boys. The whole school was called to assembly, with the newcomers to the front, to be told which class they would go into. I was placed in class A of the first-year entrants, others going into bands B and C.

We had all heard of the notorious initiation ritual known as 'the box' where all the first-years were herded into a fenced-in area of the yard and forced to run through the jeering, punching, kicking, slapping columns of seniors. Luckily I was a fast runner and got away pretty lightly; others were not so lucky.

The headmaster was Mr Drury, very keen with the cane on the backside. The deputy head was Mr Smith, an ex-pilot and our history teacher, who told us every day of his war experiences. Mr Davis No. 1 was our maths teacher, who used to throw the blackboard rubber at anyone not paying attention.

Mr Muir, our English teacher who was Irish, spoke very broad Irish, so no one could understand him. When he caned anyone, he used to gently lift your hand to the height he required with the cane and you would be expecting him come down onto the palm of your hand, but instead he would whip the cane up striking you underneath your hand, very painful.

Mr Pratt (and he was) was our woodwork teacher. The beautiful Miss Gwendolin Thomas was an English teacher whose bum wiggled when she had her back to us whilst she wrote on the blackboard. I don't know if she was being deliberately provocative but as she was only about 19 herself, she was certainly arousing many of us young boys.

Mr Bretingham was a geography teacher (we nicknamed him 'bread and jam'). He was about 22 two years of age and, like the rest of us, fancied Miss Thomas. Miss Chant was an art teacher, over 60, creaky decrepit joints and nothing like the beautiful Miss Thomas.

Then there was Mr Davis No. 2, the gym teacher. Well, as there was a Halbutt Street School for Boys, there was also a Halbutt Street School for Girls, and the schools were in one building but separated from each other. On the gym side there were three girls' classes. After a hectic session in the gym we were astonished when Mr Davis announced in a very effeminate voice, 'Right boys, shorts off and into the showers.' Many of us were pretty embarrassed by this. It's all right in the toilets trying to see if you could see who could piss over the toilet wall, but it was a different matter, being completely naked in front of everybody. However, we eventually stripped and ran into the showers only to find out later that the girls had a full view of all of us from their classrooms. One wondered longingly if Miss Thomas was there.

We never could understand Mr Davis's reasons for making us strip before we went into the shower room or why he had a satisfied smile on his face as he eyed us up and down. He obviously had a bigger smile when the sixth form showered. Anyway, all became clear when we became school-wise, if you know what I mean.

My school career was not too brilliant but I stayed in the A class throughout my schooling. My main interest at school was in sports, especially football and boxing. I knew many of the famous players of my day. It was strange, but there was one road, Bonham Road, which adjoined our road that produced vast amounts of footballing talent, going back to the likes of Dickie Walker, Jimmy Greaves and Terry Venables – a cocky, swaggering little sod, but a lovely lad! His dad and I were to become publicans together. Clive Allen and his brothers, Ken Brown, Martin Peters and many others were all from Bonham Road. The greatest of all was Alf Ramsey, the English Team Manager. He lived in a lovely very old cottage in Halbutt Street where I went to school.

Back at school, I had now managed to 'piss' over the toilet wall and become a member of the 'Behind the Bicycle Shed Smokers Club'. I think all the teachers must have been shareholders in the tobacco companies as every schoolboy, teacher and parent knew that the rarely used shed was a dog-end cemetery.

I was now playing for the school football team and training for the boxing team, having been nominated by Mr Davis No. 1. I might add that now being in the third year we had learnt, to some degree, the sexual deviations of the so-called 'shirt-lifter' Mr Davis No. 2. My younger brother Alec had now joined me in the seniors and also joined the boxing club. He was to become a brilliant boxer and fought many well-known amateur fighters of the day.

A more recent picture of my brother, Alec.

My boxing training was coming along nicely and Mr Davis No. 1 thought I was good enough to enter the English School Boys' Championship. My first fight was against a very experienced boxer, Gordon Bashford. When he entered the ring he had all the proper gear on, dressing gown, boxing boots, flashy shorts etcetera. When I entered the ring I had a grubby old towel over my shoulders, a scruffy old pair of plimsolls, and an oversized pair of shorts.

The bell rang and we sized each other up; after a few seconds of sparring he started to out-jab me. By the middle of the third round he was knocking four bags of crap out of me, so I defended my face with my gloves with my arms covering my body, waiting for the bell to ring. Sod this for a laugh, I thought, then suddenly a hell of a punch landed below the waist. I went down on my knees fighting for my breath. Thank God that's all over I thought when I had recovered; that's the first and last fight for me. But alas, it wasn't to be. As we got back to our corners, the result was announced: the winner, on a disqualification, was Eddie Cogger. Oh God, no, I thought to myself.

33

My next fight was against a boy called Adams, I forget his first name but I was pleased to see he had the same dress code that I had for my first fight. I won pretty convincingly and thought boxing wasn't so bad after all. I was now in the final of the Schoolboy Lightweight Championship of Dagenham and I was over the moon: pleased as punch, you might say. After a couple of weeks I found out that my opponent would be the existing Schoolboy Champion of Great Britain and Northern Ireland Paddy O'Callaghan.

Well, as Cassius Clay would say, he 'whupped me'. He put me down about six times, I think, but he never stopped me. I was very proud of that, as he was vastly more experienced. In fact Paddy, like me, had two brothers, Johnny and Peter. Me and my brothers fought him and his brothers on many occasions; winning some, losing some. Paddy went on to turn professional, becoming the Irish Champion.

I gave up boxing after a while and concentrated on football instead, playing for a few amateur teams, but I wasn't getting anywhere so I moved on, hoping a Miss Thomas might come along.

9

Leaving School

The end of the war saw many changes. Although things were still rationed, the shops began to stock the odd luxury, like the first banana I had ever seen, oranges, and fresh eggs instead of powdered egg. Illegal street bookmakers began to appear on street corners, as the horse and dog racing industry began to reorganise itself. The legal bookmakers had opened their businesses about a year after the war ended. Our local street bookmaker, who called himself Patsy Martin (his real name was Tommy Jennings), eventually – legally – became Harlow Bookmakers.

The police made it very difficult for the illegal bookmaker to know if the punter was genuine or a copper in plain clothes, so the bookmaker would have a stooge standing nearby. The copper, who had previously been made aware of this little charade, would cart off the dummy offender to appear in court the next day. The stooge would be fined £5 after the copper was in court to give evidence. The copper would then get his £5 later from the bookmaker. Everyone was happy, the copper with his fiver, the dummy with his fiver, the court with their fiver, but the happiest of all was the bookmaker. Now and again, however, you would get a straight copper turn up without warning and nick the bookmaker himself. Four nickings and you were banged up for six weeks.

My dad had by now nearly recovered from the severe injuries he sustained when he fell off an aircraft hangar, but he had been left very badly crippled and he sued his employers. He received a large amount in compensation for the injuries. He was made an offer which he accepted: £1,600 – in those days an enormous amount.

My dad loved a bet. One day he wrote his bet out and walked up to the corner where Tommy used to stand, but there was no sign of him. A few others were waiting for him so they asked my dad if he would give Tommy their bets when he turned up, which he said he would. Tommy never turned up ever again; he got six weeks and I believe he died sometime later. Meanwhile, my dad had now become the local bookmaker and now employed his own runners who had their own pitches (for which he paid them a percentage in the pound) and was in a strong position as he had the capital.

I, having now left school, wanted to become involved in the business and as I used to help him in his office (our front room) to settle the bets, asked him what I should do relating to my future. He said if I wanted to be involved he would write to David Cope, the biggest London bookmaker, which he did. I was asked to go to Ludgate Circus for an interview and got a job in the phone room where about 50 people, mostly women, worked answering the phones, taking the bets. My job, along with some other juniors, was to collect and stamp them.

I can recall the heavily perfumed bodily odour of 50 Miss Thomases. I was a 15-year-old in heaven. I lasted about a year but I saw no future in the job so I packed it in; my only regret was that I would finally be leaving all those Miss Thomases and their wiggly bums for good.

I then, to my parents' consternation, began to knock around with the notorious local Heathway Gang. There were two elements to this gang: the older ones who were ex-servicemen who had experienced the viciousness of war, and us younger ones who in a few years' time would be serving in the forces doing National Service.

My dad meanwhile was also becoming involved in this gang culture, mainly due to the fact that he had to have minders to protect himself from other gangs. He now went under the pseudonym of Larry Cook. He had a flash new car and all the trimmings that went with success. I remember that ours was the first house in the street to have a television. He was probably the biggest bookmaker controlling most of the Dagenham, Romford and Barking areas.

A problem did arise one day, however. He asked me to take the returns list to one of the runners, who was late. Unfortunately for me a man was strolling towards me and asked if the runner was about, and I replied 'No' and asked if he had any returns to come. The only reply I got was 'You're nicked!' as he turned out to be a plain clothes copper. As I was only aged 16 I kept my trap shut.

My dad gave me a real bollocking, as if it was my fault. Worse was to come. At the court house I was duly fined the first offender's £5, but there was a cub reporter in the room who reported on the minor cases. His two-lined report stated that Mr So and So of So and So Road, aged 18, was fined £5 for street betting. I wasn't even 18.

A week later a rebuff was printed in the local rag saying that Mr So and So of So and So Road was not the person convicted of street betting, and seeking an apology from the paper. This cost my old man lots of spondoolicks (money).

The younger members of the Heathway Gang consisted of a core of extremely violent teenagers. Many were convicted of vicious crimes, including murder, in their later years. Over the years there were many ways to describe these people: spiv, yob, wide boy, teddy boy, etcetera.

Ginger Walford was my best friend, and we used to go together to Morrie's, the hairdresser, to have our 'duck's arse' haircut and Pashana oil hair lotion massage, which I have recently rediscovered. He also went to sea with me and we also started steel erecting together. Unfortunately one day he fell and was killed.

Amongst us younger gang members was the fearsome Lennie Wiltshire, a good friend of mine who came to my aid many times later in my life when I became a publican, when I was having 'the blag' put on me. I only had to put his name up, for them to back off. We also went to sea together. He was a lovely man, but extremely dangerous.

When we were just 15 years old Lennie decided to have a tattoo. He was a hard bastard even in those days and to prove it he chose to have the biggest one he could see, and he didn't even flinch. Unfortunately for me and Ginger, he made us also have one – and I mean 'made'. I thought that my old man would do his nut but I remembered that he had one, so I looked around the shop and saw the one he had and much to Lennie's displeasure (as it was so small), I had that one.

There was Peter Penfold who served life, accused of the murder of Teddy Bear Eves, a local vender who went around the local pubs (including mine) selling toy teddy bears, hence his name. Peter was also a lovely man. There was Big H. I did not know him too well but he was also accused of the same murder. Both were also accused of burning the body in a local church, and both strongly denied these charges.

Bill Gallagher, another gang member, allegedly shot and killed a Chinaman in Singapore whilst on sentry duty at an ammunition dump whilst doing his National Service. There was a tremendous outpouring of anger from the press and public and a collection was organised to pay for his defence. However, he was charged with manslaughter and was found guilty at a court-martial and sentenced to three years in prison. The public outcry was so great that he was released after serving a short sentence. Unfortunately he couldn't handle what he had been through and began to drink; sadly he was later run over and killed.

There was Sail Smithson, strong as an ox, a really lovely young man with a captivating smile, but most dangerous if put out. He died in mysterious circumstances. He and another person had gone out in a boat on the Maplin Sands for some reason or other. The boat was later found empty. Two bodies were found tied together; it was speculated that they had got into difficulty and Sail, being a very strong swimmer, had tied the rope to both of them. An inquest delivered an open verdict.

Jerry Johnson was the first black boy I had ever set eyes on. We became great friends. He married my wife's mate and had two lovely boys. He was a good mate to keep an eye on your back but died in a car crash when under 25 years of age. He did his National Service in Malaysia.

Billy Thorn – 'Rabbits' – was nicknamed this because of his buck teeth and being the joker in the pack. Halfpenny Wilson (I never found out why he was called Halfpenny) was a good mate. Billy Baker, a hard man, was the only man who could keep Lennie Wiltshire in control and in fact I think he saved me from a terrible beating from Lennie when I first came on the scene.

Others in the gang included Dougie Alsopp and his brother Billy, who I last saw many years later selling used cars on a bomb site, typical spivs. There were many others on the periphery that would be on hand to assist if reinforcements were needed.

Saturday nights was the highlight of our week and the local Drill Hall used to put on a dance night. We used to get all suited up in our 12-inch bottoms and full drapes and display ourselves like peacocks in front of all the birds.

When I used to do boxing, skipping was a very important part of the training and one had to be very adept at this, speed being essential. On one particular night there was a jiving competition and I picked up a partner and we entered the contest. I surprised myself by showing some nifty footwork and we came second, even though the bird was a bit ropey, I thought. The winner, one of the hounds (Cockney for spiv, yob, one of the boys), was brilliant but the bird he was with was even better. He was a well-known member of the Heathway Gang, Johnny Williams, and she was a Heathway girl, Sylvia Thomas.

After a few more Saturday nights I became an expert at the jive and went in for the next competition. I knew I was good by the reaction of the crowd as they were now cheering and clapping me on. In those days it was the male who stood out, all but Sylvia Thomas: she was as good as any male dancer. On the night of the competition, I got up the courage to ask her if she would dance with me in the contest. She looked over at her regular partner, Johnny Williams, and looking back

Boxing training comes in handy for jiving.

at me she said, 'I hear you're good, yes I will.' I was well pleased with her answer and to rub his nose in it, we won.

It was at the Drill Hall that I had my first brush with the law – well, apart from the bookmaking offence, and that was down to Mr So and So of So and So Street. I, with others, was interviewed about a burglary that had occurred in the locality. It was a favourite ploy of the Old Bill to do the rounds at the local haunts primarily to get free drinks from the bar manager. After a few loutish gestures and a couple of handfuls of velvet from your teddy boy suit collar, plus a slap on your perfectly styled duck's arse hair cut, making it look more like a windswept fanny than a beautiful coiffured duck's arse, they had got what they had come for – a free pint or two – and then moved on to the next blag.

Our meeting place was outside Heathway Railway Station where we used to hang around blagging fags from anyone who passed by. I suppose in a small way, as it was in a threatening manner, it was the beginnings of demanding with intent. We then used to go on to the snooker hall, every day the same, but Saturday night was the night I looked forward to the most. It was exactly like the later film, *Saturday Night Fever*. The Drill Hall must have looked very similar to the film, sweltering heat, young men and girls sweating profusely, body odours of make-up and sex, a writhing mass of hysteria.

39

It was at this time that I got involved in a burglary. I was still only 16 and influenced greatly by this gang; I suppose I imagined I would be some sort of Humphrey Bogart or Alan Ladd.

I was told to knock on a certain door, and if anyone answered to ask if a certain person lived there. That just shows how naive I was. Anyway, no one was in so I gave them the all clear. They ran around to the back of the house, quickly broke in and opened the door. My heart was going ten to the dozen with fear, and as we entered the kitchen I nearly crapped myself at what I saw: a police sergeant's uniform hanging on the door. I ran as fast as my legs could carry me and said to myself f**k Humphrey Bogart and Alan Ladd, I'm going to join the Merchant Navy, which I did.

10

The Merchant Navy

In the month of April 1951 I went to the Merchant Navy Office in Dock Street, Aldgate East to enquire how I would be able to get into the Merchant Navy. Lennie Wiltshire and Ginger Walford came along for the ride. My friends were both sodding about and I thought they would cock it up for me. I was surprised that when the official had taken all my particulars he told me if I wanted to go to sea, I would have to do three months on a day trip boat called the *Royal Sovereign*, then I could get my Deep Sea Seaman's Passport.

Lennie and Ginger, on hearing this, asked if they would be able to do the same and got a positive response. So we were told to report to the Chief Steward on the *Royal Sovereign* (tied up at the Tower of London pier) on the morning of 10th April 1951. The *Royal Sovereign* was a pleasure boat that travelled up the Thames to Southend.

As you can guess there was some heavy drinking all day long on these trips, but not by us. They called us the heavy gang and our jobs entailed everything from humping beer barrels, washing up plates, cleaning up sick and unclogging toilets. Only when we got back to the Tower were we able to relax and go for a beer, and even then we had hassle from landlords as we were underage so Lennie, now being over 18, had to go in.

The *Sovereign* had had an interesting past. As you may know, when the Battle of Dunkirk took place, Mr Churchill sent for an armada of small ships to rescue the troops who were trapped on the beaches of Dunkirk. The *Sovereign*, along with hundreds of other small boats, some of which could only pick up four people, did their bit towards this mass evacuation.

We didn't have a lot to entertain us during this three-month training period as we were on board most of the time, dead bored. However we did have one terrifying night which brought back horrifying memories for me of the river 13 years earlier.

Certificate of Discharge.

Lennie, as was always the case, decided that we should all go swimming. The boat was tied up to four very large black buoys, two astern, two forward. We, Ginger and I, obediently following Lennie's instructions, climbed over the ship's rails and, followed by Lennie, jumped into the Thames. Not a good idea. I think we must have thought we were jumping into the local swimming pool.

In a matter of a split second I felt a terrific blow on my back and saw I had hit the buoy which had been at least 60 yards away from where I had jumped in. I saw Ginger hanging on for dear life on the other side of the buoy. The reason for this was that it wasn't the local swimming pool, it was the bleeding Thames and the tide was running at about 60 miles an hour.

We hung on to the rope for a while, gathering our breath and trying to figure a way out of the situation we were in. We eventually worked a way out of our predicament. We wrapped our arms around the rope and did the same with our legs, monkey climbing up the rope with our backs to the water and back onto the *Sovereign*. The further we climbed up the rope, the steeper the climb became as the stern of the ship was about 20 feet above the waterline. Eventually we made it. We were completely exhausted, but we had no choice, climb it or die. I had beaten a river again, the Thames.

In the meantime Lennie had been swept by the tide amongst some barges which were clanging against each other on the Bermondsey side of the river. We called out all night for him, to no avail. We didn't inform anyone of our concerns, we just hoped he would turn up, which he did, in his underpants, which was all we were wearing when we went for our terrifying swim.

Our three-month stint was soon over so I applied for my Deep Sea Book which was granted. Lennie and Ginger hadn't bothered to carry on their seafaring careers so I sailed the seven seas alone for a few more years.

The first ship I was to report to was a rusty old 6,000-ton tanker called the *Esso Bristol*. The ship was moored in the estuary at Fawley, Southampton and I had a small tender to take me to it. When it came into view my heart sank. It wasn't anything like I had expected, the smell of oil was overpowering, and the crew who were leaning over the rails didn't seem too welcoming. Getting onto the ship in itself was a disaster as I had to climb up a Jacobs's Ladder to get on board. Well, ask anyone who has had to climb one of these: it's a farce. It seemed ages as I unsuccessfully tried to master climbing this swaying, trapeze twisting, turning, as if it had life of its own. Fortunately someone took pity on me, crying out, 'Climb up sideways, son', which I did successfully. As helping hands grabbed hold of me to help me over the rails one clever bastard put his hand up my arse to lift me over the rails. Oh Lennie boy, where are you now.

My job on the *Esso Bristol* was as a galley boy, which entailed preparing the food, serving the officers, washing up the pots and pans and being prepared to do different shifts to cater for the shifts that the crew worked. Two cooks and me worked the galley, catering for approximately 30 crew who worked eight-hour shifts.

Our destination was Sidon, situated on the coast of Lebanon. We would lie up about a mile offshore, and on the sea bed would be laying the oil pipes which would be hauled up to the deck of the tanker and attached to the tanks. We would then start to fill the tanks. This procedure would take three days, the journey out would take about six days, three days loading up, and six days back to Blighty. Some hopes.

We were about four days into the return journey to Southampton and entering the dreaded Bay of Biscay. I remember standing, leaning on the rails thinking to myself of my life, of how I had settled down now as a merchant seaman, how adventurous my future would be, and I was happy within myself. I would sleep content and peaceful tonight.

I was awakened sometime in the middle of the night by what would bring absolute terror to the pit of my stomach. I heard bells ringing, loud shouting and I saw crewmen running in all directions. I couldn't fathom out what was happening so I ran out onto the tank deck. I only had my jockey pants on and, incidentally, the ship was full of oil.

I looked up to see a ship about three times the size of ours. There was a tremendous sound of steel grating against steel, the friction caused by this sent up sparks, and in my inexperienced mind I thought that these were flares sent up by our ship to take one of our crew off who might have been taken ill, or some other emergency. I saw people leaning over the rails, looking down on us. In retrospect, after I had become aware of what had happened to us, they must have thought, who was the crazy fool standing on a tank deck full of oil which was likely to explode any minute, in his jockey pants?

The sirens were now going at full blast; they were going off at three quick blasts every 20 seconds which I now know was the signal for full astern. The seaman on lookout came running down the catwalk, the bridge type construction which runs down the centre of the ship, shouting, 'We've had a collision, the bow has gone.' Almost immediately bells started ringing, hooters blowing and the Captain was on the tannoy announcing that all non-essential crew should go to midships ready to man the lifeboats.

I ran back to my cabin to get my Mae West (life jacket), ran back onto the tank deck (still in my jockey pants), panicking as I was trying to put on my life jacket whilst running up the catwalk steps. Then I was brought to a sudden stop, something was stopping me. I become aware that as I was running, the flailing tapes of the life jacket had become jammed in the structure of the catwalk.

I frantically tugged harder at the tapes, I began to panic more, sobbing as my imagination got the better of me, thinking this was the end of my short life. Then suddenly the jammed tape was released. How, I don't know how, but someone was with me that night.

I then ran along the catwalk to midships and found that the majority of the non-essential crew were sitting in the lifeboats. As I hadn't had any lifeboat training (I had only been on the ship for about two weeks), I was at a loss to know what to do. Another young man, who was the Captain's steward and obviously, like the majority of the crew, hadn't been in a situation like this himself before, told me just to sit tight and wait for instructions. It wasn't too long to wait as it became clear that we were to lower the lifeboats as there was a fire in the forward hold.

Later, as we circled the tanker we could see that the bow of the ship had been severely damaged and was burning intensely. The tanks were still holding but the rope locker was an inferno of flames and thick black smoke. The crew firemen who fought the fire were tremendously brave as they knew the tanks could explode at any moment. The ship which collided with us was watching from a safe position some distance away, in case a rescue attempt was needed, as they hadn't sustained as much damage as we had.

We in the lifeboats, had been circling the tanker for some hours when a tug arrived to assess the damage we had sustained, once the fire was out. We were very lucky that the Bay of Biscay was unnaturally calm that night and the Esso Company decided that with the aid of a deep sea tug we should be able to limp back to Southampton. We were quickly taken back on board and slowly made our way back to our home port.

When we were eventually back in Southampton and the ship was examined, we realised how lucky we had been. The bow had completely gone, leaving just a gaping hole. The ship had to go into dry dock; most of the crew were laid off, leaving just a skeleton crew and me. I had signed a six-month contract with the company and I had no option but to complete my agreement. In my first two weeks I had experienced more fear, danger and excitement than most seamen would see in a lifetime.

After I had completed the six months, the ship was still in dry dock and there was still a lot repairs to be done, so the company released me and I was on my way home. As I was travelling back to Dagenham I reflected on my life so far: the near drowning in the river at Broxbourne, the near drowning in the Thames and nearly being blown up on a tanker in the Bay of Biscay. I couldn't hardly believe it when I remembered my birth sign: with my luck it had to be Aquarius! Spooky!

After a month or so, I began to look for another ship. I had a few mates who had signed on a ship called the *Empire Windrush* which was travelling to the West Indies to pick up emigrants who were starting a new life in the UK. When I applied for a position on the ship I was told that there weren't any vacancies left which I felt very disappointed about, as I had some good mates aboard her. Anyway, my disappointment was quickly resolved when I applied and was accepted for employment on the P&O liner the *Otranto*, sailing out of Tilbury. I had quite a few friends on her as well. I was assigned to the U Gang (Utility) who basically were the heavy gang, and we got all the dirty jobs.

I hoped that the ill luck that had followed me around on my short Merchant Navy life was now in the past. However there was more bad news, although not affecting me directly. The *Empire Windrush* had caught fire on returning to the UK and many of the passengers and crew had died. She eventually sank. The *Otranto* was also an emigrant-carrying ship, taking British migrants to Australia; the fare was £10 in those days.

Our first port of call was Naples in Italy. It was my first time on foreign soil and I soaked up the atmosphere of it all. The most exciting part of the day was just as dusk was falling. I saw the spectacular sight of Mount Vesuvius with the volcano's crater glowing a brilliant red against the night sky. Everything on that journey to Australia was a wonder to me as a 17-year-old teenager.

The Suez Canal started at Port Said, and there were little bum boats from which the traders used to send their wares up on the end of a rope, shouting 'Johnny, Johnny, you buy, you buy.' The large liner only had yards to spare either side of the ship as it made its way through the canal. It amazed me how they managed to steer through such a narrow waterway. The *Esso Bristol* was tiny compared to this liner, but it still managed to collide head on in the middle of nowhere.

Our destinations included Aden, which was very primitive in those days, and Ceylon which was a beautiful pearl of an island. It was wondrous to see those enormous elephants trundling along the road on their own seemingly without a care in the world. Fremantle was our next port of call, the first port on the coast of Australia and the last one back – the local pub aptly and obviously called 'The First and Last'!

The next port was Perth, a very pretty area of Australia. Those of us who were newcomers to Australia had a very extreme culture shock at the next port of call, Port Melbourne. We arrived very early in the morning and we were surprised to see that it looked like a Wild West movie set. The sidewalks were covered in sand blown in by a gusty wind, tumbleweed bushes were caught in the wind, tumbling along as they do in the song, and most surprising of all, there were hitching rails to hitch the horses to. Or so I presumed, but no – I was wrong. Later when I had a break I went on deck for a smoke, and was surprised to see that the hitching rails were now occupied by camels.

We were allowed shore leave for the rest of the day but were not allowed to go to the city of Melbourne as this was off limits. So we had to go to the local bars, which as one might imagine were also a replica of a film set, with sawdust and spittoons. As was the norm for me I drank too much too quickly and wanted to fight everyone in sight, much to the disdain of two local Aussies in the bar.

'Want a little fight do you, sonny boy?' they asked as they grabbed me, carrying me out under their Desperate Dan muscled arms like a battering ram. They ran me through the swing doors head first, ran me across the road into the surf and dumped me into the shark-infested sea.

Drunk, defiant and bedraggled, 'You no good Aussie bastards,' I cried out to the retreating pair, desperately praying they wouldn't come back. Luckily I wasn't to be shark bait that day, as my mate Patsy Timothy came in and pulled me out. The police came and arrested me for being drunk and disorderly but they were 'fair dinkum' as they would say and they let me out after a few hours' sobering up.

In the meantime the emigrating passengers who were disembarking at Melbourne began their £10 a ticket adventure into the unknown. Our next port of call along the Australian coast was the capital, Sydney. The first thing you see as you come into Sydney is the massive bridge. The red-painted structure is enormous and made the liner look quite ordinary as she glided beneath to her berth.

When all the passengers had disembarked to the vast corners of Australia, the crew were given shore leave. I hadn't learnt anything in relation to my experience in the bar in Port Melbourne and again we headed for the nearest bar. Again I got smashed out of my head and virtually crawled back to the ship. I was told I had some near misses from being hit by the trains and lorries which were transporting goods to and from the docks. I also heard that I had upset some roughneck in the bar, who started waving a gun about.

After suffering a severe bout of DTs (delirium tremens), I decided on a lifestyle change to sort myself out. I had been in the Merchant Navy for about three years when I left, but the real reason I left was a girl, the most beautiful blonde you could see, my dearest darling Lena.

She was just 15 when I met her and had just left school and was starting her first job, selling ice creams outside a sweet shop. Of course all the lads couldn't take their eyes off this beautiful apparition of innocence, the wolf whistles bringing a tinge of a blush to her face.

Harry Wiltshire, Lennie's brother, seeing how captivated I was with her, called out to me, 'Go on Ed, ask her for a date.' Which I did.

Coyly she replied, 'I don't sell dates, only ice creams.'

My Lena.

I must have spent about five shillings on ice creams for the lads, trying to tempt her to come to the pictures with me. The only encouragement she gave me was that she would ask her parents. Unfortunately she lived at the bottom of Heathway Railway Hill where we all used to hang out. The Heathway Gang was not on most mothers' invite lists.

I began to walk her home, but being only 15 and very shy it took me weeks to ask if I could kiss her. She was mucking about picking evergreen leaves off the bush outside her house so I slowly tried to brush my lips against hers, closing my eyes as I did so. During this most amorous moment I had not noticed she had put a leaf between her lips and as my lips slightly opened, moving to receive her response, she blew the leaf into my mouth and down my throat, leaving me coughing and spluttering, laughing hysterically as she ran indoors. 'Not yet Eddie Cogger, not yet.'

Still I persevered, as Lena did, and I was invited round to see if I would be acceptable to her mum and dad and two brothers, Ernie and Benny. I went home had a bath, put on clean underwear and dressed up to the nines. First I put on my 12-inch trouser bottomed drape suit, the jacket 4 inches below the middle finger, then the suede 3-inch creepers (shoes) and finally, the crème de la crème, my hand-stitched 'guards-back' overcoat, finished off with the most lavish part of the teddy boy's make-up, his choker (scarf), crossed over his chest and twisted around his braces. My handkerchief would be a square piece of cardboard with a piece of material stitched to the top of the cardboard that was just for show. Finally, the hair: the DA (duck's arse). As there wasn't any lacquer in those days, the young men used soap to hold their hair in place by combing their hair at the back to meet together in the middle, making it look like a duck's arse, hence 'DA'. And so, ponced up like a peacock displaying itself in all its majestic glory, I set off to meet Lena's parents. I hoped the soap would hold and that I would create a good impression.

As the bus arrived at the bus stop, the usual practice of the lads, including me, was to wait for the bus to build up a head of speed and then chase after it and then leap onto the platform, grabbing hold of the handrail at the same time. The drivers were used to this and put their foot down to deter the chasers, as he did in this case. Well, my 3-inch creepers were not exactly made for chasing buses and neither was my 'guards-back' overcoat, flapping about in the wind. I nearly had my

Pashana.

arm pulled out of its socket as I just made it and fell in a undignified heap on the platform, looking a prize prat. I ran up the stairs to the laughter of all the old girls on their way to the shops.

When I got to The Heathway I popped into Morrie's the hairdressers to give myself the once-over. The barnet was OK, the soap was holding, the knees of my trousers needed a bit of a brush, otherwise everything was OK. 'Thanks Morrie, mate,' I said as I left, wondering why he had a look of horror on his face as he surveyed my hair stuck down with soap, when he had all that beautifully scented Pashana stock in his shop.

And so the moment had arrived, I was about to meet the Stovold family. Lena had explained to me (when I remarked on the unusual surname), that the name went back many centuries and that they were of Nordic stock. As I knocked on the door all dressed up like some prized turkey I felt sick to the pit of my stomach. I was 18, a member of the notorious Heathway Gang, and she, their innocent daughter, had only just left school. I felt like running away quickly. It was too late, however. The door opened and a young man with almost white blond hair stood there.

'Hello Ed,' he said, smiling broadly at me. 'Come on in and meet the family.'

I didn't know if it was my clothes or something else he was smiling at but I was so relieved to recognise him. I knew him slightly, he was about a year younger than me. Benny ushered me into the living room

Lena with her mum and two brothers – all blonde.

and I went in and saw Lena blushing, either through embarrassment or nervousness. He then introduced me to her family.

Her dad was first, and straight away all my fears evaporated, he was a lovely man and welcomed me warmly. Her mum was also welcoming but obviously wary, as any mother would be, concerned for the well-being of her daughter. She was a plump, jovial woman with a lovely disposition about her. Lena's eldest brother Ernie was the same, with a lovely way about him, always laughing. I could now see where the Nordic background came from, the mum and Lena and her two brothers Ernie and Benny had snow-white hair, while their dad had dark hair.

Now that I had broken the ice, I was feeling quite at home, although they must have thought it strange that I refused the offer to take off the 'guards-back'.

11

Courtship

Lena and I were over the moon when we got her parents' tentative permission to go out with each other. I was head over heels in love with her. In fact I was becoming so infatuated with her that her Mum began to worry, and mentioned it to her best friend who lived just around the corner to her. The friend asked her what I was like and if she knew anything of my background. She replied that I was the son of a local street bookmaker and lived on the other side of Dagenham and worked for my father. Lena's mum also said I seemed to hang about the station and the snooker hall all day long and was distracting her daughter at work. Her friend asked her what my name was and she replied, 'Eddie Cogger.'

The friend looked stunned and said, 'Queenie are you sure?'

'Yes, I am,' said Queenie.

The friend said, 'Queenie, don't you know who you're talking about? It's my young sister's son, Florrie's boy, Eddie. What a coincidence.'

It was my aunt Jess. I used to visit her quite regularly and had passed Lena's house many times before on the way to see my aunt, uncle and cousins. In fact my uncle and Lena's dad were great pals who had plots on the same allotment. She assured Queenie that I was a good lad and that she shouldn't worry.

In February 1954 I had some unwelcome news, although I had been expecting it. I was told to report to the Medical Centre at Wanstead for an examination to see if I was fit to do my National Service. I had hoped that I would be exempt from this, that the three years I had served in the Merchant Navy would count. But I realised that I would have to have served seven years to be exempt from military service.

Now Lena was in the frame, that option was a no-go. Lena by this time had changed her job; she now worked as an usherette in a local cinema. We were still madly in love with each other; I must have visited the cinema at least three times a week whilst she was there to keep my

Lena aged 17 years old.

eye on her and to make sure the yobs didn't take any liberties with her, especially when she sold the ice cream and drinks during the interval. With the spotlight shining on her, she looked absolutely beautiful.

I sought all the advice I could get to fail this exam, and the best that came up was to make out I was deaf in one ear. So came the day for the exam. There were about 20 others sitting waiting their turn. As I sat there I took a quick glance around me; everyone was very subdued. I thought that it would be better not to talk to anyone in case I made a cock-up and sodded it all up.

I saw the orderly come out of the door and quickly picked up my paper and made out to read it. 'Cogger,' he called out, but I held my head down. 'Edward Cogger,' he again called out. I still had my head down. 'Edward Cogger, I presume? Seeing you're the only one left.' I lifted my head with a mock look of surprise on my face.

'This way,' he shouted exaggeratedly, showing me to the door. Inside was a doctor, glasses hanging off the end of his nose, stethoscope dangling around his neck, looking a right berk.

'Easy peasy,' I murmured to myself.

'Close the door behind you please, Mr Cogger,' he muttered.

'Certainly,' I replied.

I knew straight away he had turned the tables on me. Balls, I said to myself. He must have thought the same to himself as he fondled mine and told me to cough, as he had done to the other 20-odd pricks who went in before me. No wonder none of us has spoken to each other; we had all made out we were deaf. It must have been a recruiting sergeant who made that one up.

A couple of weeks later I received a letter from the Recruiting Centre saying, much to my dismay, that I had passed my medical, classified A1. I had to report back for assessment as to what unit I would be going to and if I had any preference. I said I would like to join the Royal Army Transport Corp. I knew that that the Korean War was still on and the war in Malaysia as well. I thought that as I couldn't drive they would teach me, and that it was an easy number. They also asked what I had done in the Merchant Navy and I explained that I worked in the galley as an assistant pantry man.

Within a couple of months I had received my call up papers and was to report to Saint Omagh Barracks, Aldershot, on 8th April 1954. Lena and I were both gutted at this news as we would only have two weeks together before the dreaded day arrived and I had to leave her.

By now I was 20 years old and Lena was 17. We went to the cinema for the last time and saw Doris Day in *Annie Get Your Gun*. As it happens, Lena looked very much like Doris Day and when she Sang 'Once I had a Secret Love' we couldn't contain our emotions and both silently wept. If Lennie had been there he would have given me a slap, calling me a stupid bastard. Unfortunately Len was doing a two-year stretch in Borstal. Lena and I said our tearful goodbyes sitting on the stairs of her parents' passageway, then I had to leave her.

When I got to the station on the way home, all the faces were there – Ginger, Sail, Rabbits, the Baker brothers etcetera, all taking the piss by chanting 'No DA this time tomorrow' and 'You're in the Army now'. The next day I was to present myself at Saint Omagh Barracks, home of the Army Catering Corps, the ACC.

12

The Army Catering Corps

I made my way to the train which was to take me to Aldershot Station. The station was absolutely packed with young men, the majority dressed like me, teddy boys. Aldershot was the home of the British Army and most of the battalions and corps were trained there before they moved on to their home or overseas deployments.

At the start of our journey to Aldershot all the National Service men were segregated into their own carriages, in our case the carriage for the ACC, and given instructions as to what the procedure would be when we got to Aldershot Station. The people in charge seemed to scream out every instruction they gave, and anyway most of us didn't know what they were on about, but one thing we did prick up our ears to was something about haircuts which drew a loud response of booing. The screamers went ballistic.

We eventually arrived at our destination, Saint Omagh Barracks. There were about a hundred of us and we were marched at what the screamers called 'the double' into a gym, lined up at arm's length apart, and told to strip. We began to look coyly around at each other and then it started. The screamers (I have to call them that as we didn't know what rank or who they were, having only been in the army a few hours) started 'in your face' tactics. A few of the really hard men didn't like this approach so retaliated by sticking their nut into the offending face. They were whisked away by the Military Police, who were standing by as this must have been a common occurrence on these enlistment days.

Slowly we began to strip, then faster as the ear-bashing began. So the humiliation started. 'Right you horrible lot' (they all start with that) 'spread your legs apart and bend over.' Oh god not that, I said to myself. I had gone three years in the Merchant Navy and it looked as if I was about to lose my cherry to some spotty little Lance Corporal in three minutes. However, it was not to be. I felt a spray of something up my arse, waited apprehensively and was told to turn around. I saw this instrument and realised it was a DDT spray can: we were all being sprayed for crabs.

Next was the dreaded visit to the barbers. They could have earned a fortune as sheep shearers – all off in 30 seconds. My beautifully coiffured DA lay on the floor like a dead cat, and the barber then took the piss by holding a mirror up to my bald head with a little tuft on the top asking, 'Will that be all right, sir?'

Next stop was the outfitters. Looking you up and down they would guess your size for your uniform: 36-inch chest, 29-inch inside leg, size 8 boots hanging around your neck and big floppy beret stuck on your head, etcetera. They had so many to sort out over the years I suppose it was second nature to them now.

Now here I was, in the Army, Private 23018587 Edward L. Cogger, pissed off, sick as a pig and lovesick for my darling Lena, who I wouldn't be seeing until I had finished my training in six months' time. My first inclination was to have it away; I couldn't stand this for two days let alone two years. I could go back in the Merchant Navy, I still had my passport and I could jump ship in Australia. But what about my Lena? I couldn't leave her. So I decided to stay put and take the medicine, and there was plenty of that.

We were then marched to our barracks and told to put our kit on our allocated bed, and it was then that the legendary orders started:

First week in the Army – I'm standing third from right.

58

'Stand by your beds you slovenly load of crap, stand to attention, stand at ease.' It was never-ending. Eventually it stopped, and a gleaming NCO (non-commissioned officer) then announced, 'I am the Sergeant in charge of you horrible lot', in a thick Scottish accent. 'Sergeant MacVie is my name. Corporal Dean and Lance Corporal Riley are my subordinates.' So we could now put a handle on the screamers.

Still in our civvies, minus overcoats and jackets, we were ordered to go outside at the double and line up in rows of four. If that sounds difficult, you should have seen the state we got in when the order to right turn was given. It was hilarious; some about turned, others left turned, and others didn't know what way to turn at all and stayed as they were, what a cock-up. Eventually we got to face the way we were to go and marched off in a most undisciplined fashion, much to the disapproval of Lance Corporal Riley, or 'Old Mother Riley' as he later became known. However, he had the last laugh as he knew where he was taking us to, the Medical Department for our jabs – three of them, and one that separated the men from the boys. Cor blimey, it didn't half hurt. We were marched back to our billet again; arms swinging less obviously this time, and later were marched to the canteen to eat and to see what our function would be in the future when we were fully trained up to be cooks and chefs in the Army Catering Corps.

First and foremost though, we were soldiers, and had to go through the same basic training and discipline as any other soldier. The first day we were awoken by someone playing the trumpet – later we learnt it was a bugle playing reveille, a military waking signal – immediately followed by a series of loud shouts, screaming, dustbin lids being clashed together and cries of 'Get out of your pits, you wankers, stand by your beds, you're in the Army now.' 'Private Cogger stop scratching your balls, Private Scott open your f***ing eyes, you're still asleep.' Etcetera, etcetera. It was Sergeant MacVie and his two henchmen Dean and old Mother Riley.

After all the pleasantries had been seen to, we were shown how to make our pits (beds) according to Army regulations, how to iron, how to lay out our kit, measured with a ruler, how to pick it all up once the Sergeant had flung it to all corners of the barrack room until it met with his satisfaction.

Next came the boots, what a palaver, if I can recall it correctly 50-odd years on. We used to put boot polish into a spoon put the spoon over a lighted candle and when the polish had melted, we then poured the polish over the toecap of the boot. When it was dried we then,

Me: 'They don't like it up them Capt. Mainwaring.'

using a very soft cloth, began to polish the toecap starting with very small circles until we had gone all over the toecap. We would then spit on the toecap and polished it until a highly polished sheen appeared, hence I presume this is where 'spit and polish' originated from.

We also had a second set of uniforms called 'fatigues', meant for everyday work and training exercises. One of the most important tasks we had was to shrink the extremely large and floppy beret we were given to wear, as it was absolutely stupid. The method we used to shrink them was to soak them in hot water for an hour or so and then plunge them in cold water. This was usually successful after two or three times.

We heard the trumpet (sorry, bugle), play again; everyone knew this even if they hadn't been in the cake (Army) before: 'Come to the cookhouse door, boys. Come to the cookhouse door', the cookhouse being a restaurant where everyone ate. The bugle was played at first light to get out of bed (reveille), then three times a day for food, then for lights out (bedtime).

The first week seemed to last an eternity; we seemed to spend forever on the parade ground mastering the art of walking, or in military jargon, 'marching'. It was absolutely pathetic; some swung both arms together, some not at all, others couldn't march in step together. Sergeant MacVie, Dean and old mother Riley had a field day trying to rupture a few eardrums. Finally after a few weeks, we began to get it all together and all the individual companies A, B, C etcetera (which had been training separately) began working together as a battalion, in readiness for the Queen's Birthday Parade, under the infamous RSM Britain, the most legendary Regimental Sergeant Major in the British Army.

But first we had to endure the bullying that our own NCOs were putting us through. One particular Company Sergeant Major was a really nasty piece of work, and one young lad was always on jankers for insubordination. The lad couldn't take any more and told the Sergeant to 'Stick it up your arse' and started to walk off the parade ground. He was immediately collared by three of the 'ear perforators' and marched to the guardhouse.

The Company Sergeant Major then issued this warning to us all: 'If I have any more of this insubordination, I will have you running around this parade ground in ever-decreasing circles until you run up your own arse.'

I lost it then, imagining someone running up their own arse. I was hysterical. Others joined in then, and then the whole company started.

'Right you horrible shower, you are all confined to barracks for a week, we will see who has the last laugh,' he said. He did: every order had to be done at the double, our bedding and kit were strewn asunder, jankers handed out for the least misdemeanour ... it was a long week.

The day of the Queen's Birthday arrived; we were awoken by the sound of reveille, marched to the cookhouse and then after breakfast back to the billet to prepare for this special event. We were then inspected by the commanding officer and when all was satisfactory we were loaded onto lorries and driven to where the event was being held, a massive sports area which led all the way to Aldershot. There were selected companies from all the battalions based in Aldershot. We were all lined up one arm's length apart in our individual companies, and there were about 2,000 of us.

Suddenly a staff car drew up, and as it did all the Company Sergeant Majors of the battalions present brought their companies to attention. The car door opened and the most awesome man I had ever seen stepped out. He was immaculate from head to toe, the infamous Regimental

Sergeant Major Britain, from his peaked cap down to his bristling moustache, his uniform fitting his portly body perfectly with his red sash and his highly polished belt and buckle gleaming in the sunlight. His creased trousers looked as sharp as razors and his boots looked as though many years of spit and polish had been devoted to them. Six foot two of him, striding towards the rostrum, back as stiff as a poker, the senior NCO in the British army, Guardsman RSM Britain was to conduct the ceremony on the Queen's Birthday. I could not believe the power of his voice as he brought 2,000 men to attention, it was overwhelming. I had (although being anti-authority at the time) great respect for him.

The time came for us to step up our skills now that we were entering a new phase in our training. So after we finished our square-bashing, we then had to go on the rifle range. On the rifle range we trained with the Enfield rifle. I think we had a dozen shots at a target and I can't remember if I even hit the target. The second day we used the Sten gun, single shots first and then stand at ease, Sten gun at your side and then prepare for quick bursts.

Suddenly there was a tirade of screaming and shouting: 'Cogger, you haven't got your f***ing safety catch on, you'll blow your bleeding foot off in a minute.' I quickly rectified that.

I had by now acknowledged that I had to settle down and get on with it and hope that the two years would fly by. We were now a really well trained unit, unrecognizable from the rabble that turned up on that first day and were told that the 12 smartest turned out men would be chosen for guard duty. Having spent weeks training with the Enfield perfecting all the various rifle exercises, we were called to the parade ground for the smartest dozen men to be selected for the first sentry duty of the company. Two officers were inspecting the company (one of them was Billy Butlin's son, the holiday camp king). When they got to me, I was well pleased to be selected as one of those who would be on guard duty that night.

Those of us who were chosen were dismissed from the rest of the company and told to report to the armoury to pick up our rifles and report back to the Guard Commander and the two officers, who would inspect us again. When it got to my turn I was brought to attention and inspected from my highly polished cap badge down to boots that you could see your reflection in.

'Name?' one inquired of me.

'Private Cogger, sir,' I shouted back.

'Good effort,' he replied, and moved on to the next one, leaving me feeling very smug indeed.

It wasn't to last long. Next came rifle inspection, a procedure where you come to attention, your right leg moves back a pace and you put your thumb in the breech, bring the rifle up to the inspecting officer's eyes so it enables him to see down the barrel to the thumb nail and gives him a clear view to see if it is in pristine condition.

The officer (Billy Butlin) called the Sergeant to him and said, 'Sergeant, put this man on a charge, dirty rifle.'

I tried to explain that I hadn't even seen the rifle before, and was put on another charge for answering back to an officer.

I was brought up in front of the CO, and I again tried to explain to him that the rifle had come straight out of the armoury. Anyway, it

'Get your hair cut!'

63

seems that even intelligent men like him just go into this mode of stupidity, as we all did eventually. I ended up getting seven days confined to barracks. This meant I had to report to the guardroom three times a day, in full dress with back pack, with all the others who had fallen foul of something or someone; they would get you one way or another.

My confinement to barracks was to last 14 days; for some reason they kept finding fault with my mess cans (what our food was put in). Finally I finished jankers and the 12 weeks of military training was over; we were now going on to train to be cooks. This was to last another 12 weeks and then we would be transferred to our battalions.

I took to cooking very well, mainly due to the struggle I had when I was a youngster. I had to duck and dive when my dad was on the brink of death, to help my mum and two brothers through the last years of the war. So I came through the ACC's training courses with distinction, a B class cook and a temporary Lance Corporal's stripe. I had been allocated to join the Lancashire Fusiliers in Iserlohn in Germany but first I was going home on two weeks' leave to see my darling Lena.

It had been a long six months for us both but the almost daily love letters we wrote to each other kept our passion for each other as strong as ever. On my return I telephoned Lena and told her I was home and would be straight around to see her. As I passed the Heathway Station a lot of the 'hounds' were standing outside the station just as it was before. The 'deaf in one ear' job must have worked for them, I thought. As I got to Lena's front door and looked through the glass panel I thought I saw Lena coming to open the door, but after a short delay her dad appeared. 'Hello son,' he said. 'Come on in.'

There she was, my beautiful Lena, standing in front of me. For a moment I wasn't sure if she was going to shake hands with me; seeing that her dad was standing there I thought she might have been embarrassed, but we had a little peck on the cheek.

Later when we were alone I asked her if it was her I had seen through the glass of her front door when I knocked. She said it was, but she had thought the image she saw through the window was rather comical: no hair, no big shoulders, just a skinny little me and she felt too embarrassed to open the door, which on reflection was right. We have had a good laugh when we have recollected those memories over the years.

My dad was still running a book but was having a problem with opposition from another bookmaker called Mark Lane who began operating on the other side of Dagenham. My dad was operating his business on the Chadwell Heath side of Dagenham which was controlled by Chadwell Heath police station. It was no surprise that some of the police in those days were as bent as the villains. They would call at our house on Sunday mornings and give my dad information on the day that they would be carrying out a raid on his pitches so that he could put up ringers (as I have previously explained). Obviously this information wasn't free, but my dad had no choice but to pay, otherwise they would be nicking him every day.

Then the other side of the coin would turn up, the villains, coming for their piece of the cake. They came in handy at times. I remember that on one occasion my dad had his very expensive Crombie overcoat nicked from his local pub, the Cherry Tree in Wood Lane, Dagenham. Apparently the villains – probably the same ones who paid my dad a visit every Sunday morning – found out that the person who had nicked my dad's coat was visiting a friend in hospital. They paid him a visit. I understand he was in hospital a lot longer than his friend; a slip of the razor, I believe he told the police.

My two weeks' leave seemed to pass so quickly, and I thought of going 'on the trot' as I was that desperate not to leave my Lena, but I realised that no matter how long I had it away for I would still have to do the time. The time came when I had to return to training camp and leave my lovely Lena. Every lover experiences an ache in their heart when they leave their loved one and I was no exception, I hurt terribly.

When I got back to the barracks we were given our embarkation orders. I was destined to go to the Lancashire Fusiliers, serving in the Army of Occupation of Germany. Others were going to Korea, Malaysia and other bases around the world. The day eventually came when we left the training company at Saint Omagh and were transported by lorry and ferry to the Hook of Holland and then by train to our individual destination, in my case Iserlohn, Germany.

A lorry was sent to meet me at the station and I was most surprised to see that it was being driven by a German, who was wearing the same uniform and cap that you would see on the newsreels at home when they surrendered.

'Kinder Cogger?' he asked, I didn't know what 'kinder' meant but as I was the only squaddie there I presumed he meant me. I later learnt he was taking the piss, 'kinder' meaning child.

I was dropped off at the guardhouse of the Lancashire Fusiliers and I then realised I was now in the proper Army. I walked into the guardroom with my kitbag over my shoulder, suitcase in my hand, dead

Me – on the right.

knackered, to ask who I had to report to, to be met by a tirade of abuse.

'You scruffy f***ing piece of shit coming into my guardhouse looking like a f***ing splattered fart, get outside and tidy yourself up.' That was my introduction to the Sergeant of the Guard of the First Battalion XX Lancashire Fusiliers.

After I was eventually allowed to leave the guardroom, one of the guards escorted me to my quarters and I met the rest of the cooks. Corporal Stott was the senior NCO on duty and told me what my duties would be the following day. I would be meeting the ACC Sergeant; apparently he was an alcoholic with an attitude. That was all I needed.

After a restless sleepless night – fear, no doubt – I followed the rest of the cooks to the cookhouse. There was one advantage of getting up before reveille: no parade and no inspection, I felt a lot better now. Corporal Stott was the first to arrive to relieve the night duty cook, who had prepared the breakfasts for the battalion – 1,001 men, the odd man being the Colonel – at least I knew that. I, having been used to cooking for large groups, soon settled in and was directed to work with another cook called Nobby Clark, like me a Cockney.

The Sergeant came into the cookhouse just before breakfast, saw me and called me over.

'I suppose you're Cogger,' he stated. 'Regular or National Service?'

'National Service, sir,' I replied.

'Sergeant to you, lad, I am not one of those nancy boy two-year National Service Officers. I am a 21-year regular, got it?'

'Yes, Sergeant,' I replied.

I could see I would have to be very careful dealing with him; he could be very dangerous, especially when he got drunk – practically every day in the Sergeants' Mess. His bloated mauve face made it obvious that he was an unpredictable alcoholic.

I turned back to Nobby, who told me he was a seven-year regular and had only been there himself for two weeks. We, being the only two Cockneys in the battalion, struck up a close friendship. He was a lovely lad. The Lancashire Fusiliers were basically all regulars and were a mixture of Scousers (natives of Liverpool) and Mancunians (natives of Manchester).

After about three months, Nobby and I had settled in and decided to make our first foray into the NAAFI (the bar). Most of the cooks who weren't on duty used the bar most nights of the week, especially Nobby and I. We were about 5 miles from Iserlohn city so we just knocked about the NAAFI, drinking all the time. Although I was only 20 I could hold my drink, having served my drinking apprenticeship in the Merchant Navy and the pubs at home.

Also, I could look after myself, which was down to Lennie Wiltshire who on one occasion, hearing someone taking the piss out of me, told me to nut him. Well I had done some boxing but no street fighting. Lennie left me in no doubt what he would do to me if I didn't. So I did as I was told, and as I didn't know how to nut anybody I just dived head first at him, striking him a terrific blow in the face, nearly knocking myself out. He went down, and as I was reeling about I heard Lennie shouting, 'Put the boot in, Ed, put the boot in.' F***k this for a laugh I thought, as I struggled to sort him out from the stars spinning in my head. They were exactly the same stars that I saw when Paddy O'Callaghan beat the shit out me in the Dagenham School Boys' Championship.

Anyway I didn't cop one off Lennie and we walked away, arms around each other's shoulders, me still sorting my head out from the stars and laughing at the poor bastard lying in the crucifixion position, probably feeling much worse than I did with my trip to the stars.

13

Promotion

After I had been in Germany for about two months I was told to report to the Sergeant. Having just come back from the Sergeants' Mess he was well gone, and he could hardly speak. 'Clark,' he blabbered, a mixture of foam and spit running down the corner of his mouth. Nobby and I were sick and tired of his confusing us – I suppose it was our Cockney accents – and usually just let him get on with it. I tried one more time,

'Sergeant, my name is Cogger.' I spelt it out for him, 'C O G G E R.'

In his drunken stupor he ended up with 'Clargger' coming out of his addled mouth. 'I am recommending you to go on an NCO's cadre.'

I was taken aback at this as I thought he didn't like me. I thought this was rather strange and then I realised it must be because I now

My scones didn't rise!

played football for the battalion. I had scored five goals the previous Saturday which had put the team into the final of the BAOR cup and the Army, which tended to look after their sportsmen, were sending me on a cushy course to wrap me up in cotton wool to avoid me going on any dodgy manoeuvres.

The two courses I was going on were a 'B3' Cooking Course and a 'B2' junior NCO's course. I passed both but I was held back for another week because my f***ing scones didn't rise. When I got back to the battalion I was put on orders and the Colonel questioned me on why my scones never rose.

'Not enough yeast, sir,' I replied.

Bleeding heck, I thought, what a stupid question. However, he gave me a mild rebuke and then presented me with my full Corporal's stripes. What a load of bullshit, just for playing football. I never got picked for the final anyway. I wasn't a real soldier, just a cook who happened to be attached to the 1st Battalion XX The Lancashire Fusiliers. I would get my own back on the bastards that night: an extra gob in the chip fryer would do the trick. That's how you know if the fat's at the right temperature for cooking: the spit bounces along the top of the boiling oil.

14

The Wrong Man

The Cook Sergeant called me into his office the following day to give
me a bollocking, asking why I was seven days late in returning to camp.
I tried to explain the farcical scone/yeast episode but he was still suffering
from last night's binge, so I didn't bother trying to explain any more.

However he did congratulate me on my promotion: 'Anyway, well
done Corporal Clark.' Here we go again, I thought. 'At least we should
look after our regulars, not those no-good bastard National Servicemen.'
I was about to correct him when I realised that he really did think I
was Clark. The stupid drunken prick had promoted the wrong man. I

The Wrong Man. Corporal Clargger, Clogger ... I don't know but I got 'The Stripes'.

bet Clarkie's f***ing scones would have risen with or without yeast. Shit I am in it now, I thought.

What could I do now? I could get court-martialled for impersonating an NCO. My brain was spinning. Who could I turn to? Stupid git of a piss artist Sergeant, he had really put me in the shit now. I thought of Corporal Stott: we had got on pretty well; he lived in married quarters with his wife and three kids.

Corporal Stott advised me to let things carry on as they were, don't tell Clarkie anything about it, just let the Sergeant carry on believing I was a regular until I finished my time, It was hard shit for Clarkie, but he had another five years to perfect his King Alfred role, while I had only about 14 months to go and my Lena wouldn't wait indefinitely for me.

We used to go on manoeuvres frequently and one of them was held at Hamlin where the Pied Piper was supposed to have been promised a reward to rid the village of a plague of rats by playing his pipes and luring the rats into the river (which is why we were there, to do a river crossing). However the villagers reneged and whilst they slept, the Pied Piper played his pipes, lured the children into the caves, and they were never seen again. Grimm stuff!

As you may know, or not, Army infantry battalions are made up of companies A, B, C etcetera, HQ and the motor pool. Each company has a Major in charge and junior officers, NCOs and the ordinary ranks. HQ Company is positioned about a mile behind the front line and the position is defended by troops consisting of signallers, drivers, the bandsmen, the cooks (I wondered why I had that Enfield rifle which I had only ever fired 12 shots from) and 'Uncle Tom Cobley an' all'.

When the companies had all dug in at their allocated positions, the cooks had to set up their equipment ready to start cooking. My equipment consisted of two very large Bunsen-type burners which were placed either end of a trench, upon a structure like a tunnel, which the cooking bins were placed on, the burners facing each other.

I left the cook (who was assisting me) to look after things whilst I took a trip around the individual company cookhouses to see how they were progressing in setting up their field cookhouses. As I was on my way back to my own kitchen I heard a tremendous explosion coming from the direction of my cookhouse. I saw two plumes of smoke rising from where the burners had been, cooking bins strewn asunder, and an Al Johnson look-alike of a cook's smoke-covered face as he ran around in a state of panic, nearly shitting himself.

'F***ing hell,' I said. 'What did you do?'

'Me, you stupid bastard? It was you, you left the two burners facing each other and they have set fire to each other.'

F**k, I said to myself. I had been trying to be so clever, trying to cut corners by putting the two burners facing each other, and I forgot to regulate them. Luckily for me the company was in the field, playing at Dad's Army, and had their field rations taken to them by transport. They must have thought that live ammunition was being used when they heard my explosion. I ducked and dived and managed to get hold of another two burners, although the Quarter Master must have had the surprise of his life to find two badly damaged burners in his stores. Having two stripes comes in very handy, in this case it's who you know, not what you know and the Corporals' Mess is a handy place where favours are quickly returned, especially by the Cook Corporal.

Me and my kitchen equipment – which I blew up!

Headquarters Company, being the nerve centre of the battalion, was at the rear of the battalion and was controlled by the Colonel and the staff officers. The senior non-commissioned officer was Regimental Sergeant Price. Rumour has it that before they came to Germany, the battalion which was based in Aden came under attack by insurgent Arabs and RSM Price distinguished himself by tying a body to the bonnet of his jeep and driving around camp, showing off the body.

When you are on manoeuvres it is basically training for war. Obviously you must have an enemy, which in this case was the Royal Leicestershire Battalion and a Canadian regiment. We were supported by the Welsh Fusiliers (Welsh again, funny old world) and a tank regiment.

We, the cooks, had finished for the night and began to settle down in our bivouacs (a very small tent-like covering) for the night. The sentries were patrolling the perimeters and it was very quiet considering the amount of men and equipment in the area. I was lying in my bivouac, and it was an absolutely freezing night: I had on my uniform and my heavy overcoat, and a trench coat covering me, and was still freezing.

I was just about to drop off to sleep when I heard a loud bang and looking up I saw a brilliant glare in the sky, gently floating down – I realised it was a flare. At the same time pandemonium broke out, with whistles blowing, men shouting out orders – absolute chaos. We were ordered by RSM Price to take cover under the lorries with our rifles and shout 'Bang', as we didn't have any blank bullets, like the proper soldiers did. I ask you, 'Bang!'

Anyway none of us won, as the manoeuvres ended a couple of days later when a little rocket exploded in the sky and was deemed to be an atom bomb so we were all popped off.

15

Back to Barracks

When we eventually got back to camp I returned to the cookhouse to report back for duty. Corporal Stott told me that I had to report to the Colonel immediately. I convinced myself that I was going to be court-martialled for impersonating an NCO. F**k it, that stupid bastard of a piss arse of a Sergeant has really dropped me in the shit now. Or that perhaps the Quarter Master Sergeant had found those two badly wrecked burners smuggled into his stores. I smartened myself up and reported for COs orders.

'Corporal Cogger, I have had a request for you to be allowed compassionate leave. Your mother has been taken very seriously ill in childbirth so I will send you home with a two-week pass with immediate effect. Good luck.'

I returned to my quarters, quickly packed, and within two hours was on a train to the Hook of Holland. I was so grateful that the Cook Sergeant was still a drunken slob and the Quartermaster Sergeant hadn't yet found the two wrecked burners he had in his stores. But I had much more to worry about than those two old farts: right now my mum was my biggest concern.

I was well pleased to know that I would be seeing my Lena tomorrow. The journey took about eight hours to the Hook of Holland and then I had to take a ferry to England, arriving the following morning, then it was a couple of steam train journeys and the Tube to Heathway Station, Dagenham.

As I walked up the station ramp I wondered if any of the gang would be there. Sure enough some of them were, Rabbits, Halfpenny Wilson, the Baker brothers and a few hanger-ons. They were surprised to see me and asked if I was on the trot. I explained the situation relating to my mum, and they wished her well. I moved on, looking down the hill to Lena's house. I hadn't had the opportunity to inform her that I was getting compassionate leave when I left, so she was probably at work.

I arrived home to find my dad in a right old state. My two younger brothers Alec (who would be going into the Army himself next year) and Barry were doing their best to console him. As I understood it, my mum was seven months pregnant and she and the baby were both in danger and it looked as if the baby was going to be born prematurely.

When I got home the first thing I did was to ring Lena, who was shocked to learn I was home. I explained my mum's situation and said that I would see her later. I would be seeing my darling Lena soon.

I went to see my mum later that day and although she was very ill she was so pleased to see me. The next day she gave birth to a two-months premature baby girl. As she was so sick and it wasn't sure if she would make it, she was christened straight away, Catherine Ann. She weighed in at 3 pounds and 7 ounces. Thank God, my mum began to recover slowly after that. My baby sister was born on 12th March 1955; that meant I had one year and one month more to do in the Army.

I rushed from the hospital as quickly as I could to see my sweetheart. I had some niggling doubts in my mind as to her feelings for me, as she had only just left school when I first saw her at the ice cream stall; I was now 21 and she was 17, and I thought she might have just had a schoolgirl crush on me. We had sent love letters to each other regularly, but in six months things can change.

As I knocked at the door my stomach was churning, and my heart was doing that unexplainable thing that it does when you are madly in love. I saw the curtains twitch, heard a little screech, footsteps running down the passage, the door flew open and there she stood, my beautiful little Lena. We immediately hugged and kissed each other, both tearful with emotion. Although she had matured, she was still the little girl who had blown a leaf down my throat, nearly choking me, when I tried to sneak my first kiss ('Not tonight Eddie Cogger, not tonight').

Lena and I were inseparable during those two wonderful weeks we had together; our love for each other was overwhelming. She had such a romantic way about her, and being a usherette in the cinema, she seemed to imagine that she was the beautiful heroine of a film. To my love-filled heart, she was.

Whilst I was at home we spent most of our time together, but I did have a night off as Lena wanted to wash her hair so I decided to go to the Heathway to see the lads before I returned to Germany. They were all there, about 20 of them. It appeared that they were on their way to a pub called The Fanshawe, as they had been in an incident the previous week when one of the boys had been badly beaten up. Foolishly, I agreed to go along. Some were tooled up, others were carrying wooden staves. It looked like a battle royal was about to take place. We gathered at the end of the bar, backs to the bar, so there wouldn't be any attack from behind. As we were sussing each other out, I saw my dad walk into the pub.

'What are you doing here, Dad?' I asked him.

'There's been an emergency with the baby, she's got meningitis, and we've got to go the hospital,' he said.

I explained the situation to the lads, wished them well, and shot off to the hospital as quick as possible. My mum and dad were devastated by this latest tragedy to hit our family. First my dad crippled for life, now my week-old baby sister fighting desperately to cling on to life. After staying at the hospital for about four hours with the baby still critical but no worse, my dad told me to go home to get some rest, and to come back the following morning.

In the early hours of that next morning I heard a terrific hammering on the front door. Thinking that it was bad news about the baby I rushed down the stairs and on opening the door my heart sank, it was the police. 'Oh my God', I cried out, repeating over and over again. 'Not the baby.'

My two brothers, hearing all the palaver, came down also expecting the worst. Instead, the police officers asked me my name, which I gave them.

'Edward Lawrence Cogger, you are under arrest for, with others, causing an affray resulting in the attempted murder of the [injured person's name], anything you say' etcetera, etcetera. F**k me, I thought to myself, 'murder', 'affray' what's all this about?

When I got to the police station I was questioned as to my whereabouts on the previous evening. As I wasn't aware of anything going off at the pub, I said I was at the pub for about an hour and then explained the emergency we had with my baby sister and that I had been at the hospital all night. Apparently there was a right battle royal when I left for the hospital and one of the other gang (a copper's son) got badly slashed in the throat, seriously injuring him. Many on both sides were also hurt but not so badly as he was. It took a lot of convincing the Old Bill that I wasn't there at that particular time, but with cast iron witness statements from the doctors and nurses they had to accept this.

I wasn't home when about six of the lads went on trial charged with the lesser offence of causing an affray; they got an average of six months each. The police couldn't prove who did the actual slashing but luckily the wounded person survived or it could have meant some unlucky bastard having a date with Mr Harry Allen (the hangman) – remember, he was still about then. I was 30 years old when he hanged his last convicted murderer and the death penalty was abolished.

The final week of my leave seemed to fly by, Lena and I were both dreading the day we had to leave each other again. Apart from the hospital emergency and the fight in the pub, we had had a beautiful romantic time. Although my baby sister took a lot longer to get well and was kept in hospital a lot longer than mum, they both eventually came home.

16

Back to Camp

I arrived back at camp to find that the Cook Sergeant wanted to see me. I still had this compulsive idea in my head that he would find out that I was not a regular. However, that wasn't the case: he explained that the Night Corporal was due for demob and that he would be putting me in that position. What a stroke of luck I thought. It was a dead cushy number; I would rarely see the drunken old bastard now. I would be in my pit all day if I wanted to as no one could go in the night cook's room; no inspections, no manoeuvres, early nights in the NAAFI, I was in heaven. Just one setback: we shared our quarters with the battalion drummers, so I would have to get some ear plugs as they practised on window sills, doors, anything that came to hand, when they weren't on the parade ground.

So I set about my new duties, which entailed preparing all the morning's breakfasts and overseeing the serving up of the meals. The catering set-up in the Army is quite simple, and the rations are laid down in stone by the nutritionist, for example 4 ounces of meat a week, six potatoes a week, four eggs ... anyway, you get the drift of what I am getting to. If someone tries to nick an extra spud, or egg or bacon, the squaddies who are at the back of the queue would get nothing, so a sharp rap on the knuckles with a serving ladle soon deters them. One particular bastard was always at it and a really nasty hatred developed between us; however, more of that later.

I was really happy with the situation I was now in and I was more relaxed knowing everything was well at home; my baby sister had survived her difficult start to life. My love for my darling Lena was true, and hers for me.

Lena with my lovely little sister Tina, now recovering from her meningitis.

17

Last Leave Before Demob

I was now on my final last six months before demob. My darling Lena had now matured into a beautiful young woman, and we were inseparable.

My dad was having problems with his bookmaking business: apart from the police giving him lots of hassle and Mark Lane, the other bookmaker on the other side of town seemingly having a hassle-free ride from the police, he was finding it difficult to carry on. He had to sell his flash car and had to go around his pitches by bike which he found very humiliating; he had even taken my annuity grants that servicemen have to send home as a form of savings for their future when they leave the forces.

The Heathway Gang were still very much part of my life, Lennie was unquestionably the top man: vicious, fearless, he demanded loyalty to the extreme and wouldn't stop at badly hurting anyone who didn't go along with this. Lena wasn't particularly concerned with my association with them, she was so young and innocent, and she probably thought she was playing the part of a gangster's moll in a film at the cinema where she worked.

I knew her mum wasn't so keen on me, 'He won't come to much, hanging about that station and snooker hall all day long,' she used to say.

Her dad used to like me though: 'He's a nice boy,' he used to say. He served in the Army during the war and was in the landings at Dunkirk, going right through the war. He suffered terribly from emphysema at the end and was severely disabled. He loved a uniform, though, and he was so proud to be British, especially when his two sons did their National Service. We were in the Army at the same time: Ernie in Italy, Bennie in Hong Kong and me in Germany.

Well, it was now time to leave my loved one for the last time. The next time I saw her I would be a free man. We said our loving goodbyes, and as I got to the station I turned, saw her with her bobbed blonde

Lena's dad.

hair standing outside her house, waved to her, and walked into the station.

'Got a fag, Ed?' said some lone prick standing outside the station.

'F**k off.' I was in no mood for a wanker like that at this time.

18

Back to Camp for the Last Time

I arrived back at the barracks around midday, reported to the guardhouse, and had a laugh with the RPs (Regimental Police) – who are different from the MPs (Military Police). They were taking the piss, saying that now that I was back, they would be back on shitty food now. They used to call me 'Coggee'. Jokingly they mocked, 'Coggee's back, we will all have f***ing food poisoning by tonight.' F***ing right, I said to myself, I will have a right old gob in the cooking oil tonight, the bastards.

I wandered over to the cookhouse to see how the lads were getting on. Nobby was on duty with some of the other cooks and I was surprised to see he had been promoted to Lance Corporal.

'What's been happening here, Clarkie?' I said, flicking his stripe. 'Where's the Sergeant?'

'He had a f***ing heart attack, scared the shit out of me. They have shipped him back home,' he replied.

'Who's in charge,' I asked, hoping to God he wouldn't say me. It would just be like the f***ing old bastard to do that to me.

'Corporal Stott is in charge during the day as he lives in married quarters, with me as his Lance Corporal and you carry on as Night Corporal. A new Sergeant is arriving next week.'

At least the old bastard hadn't found out about the mix-up between our identities and anyway it was only right that Nobby should only get one stripe, he might have another five years to do after I leave but I had the problem of not getting my scones to rise. I will be in the shit in later years if a certain part of my anatomy fails to rise like those poxy scones didn't.

I thought I would pop in the NAAFI for a drink before I had to go on duty. As was the norm now I was beginning to drink quite a lot as the Night Cook's job was a really cushy number, and I had no one to answer to. The only people I saw were the RPs who came in to collect the prisoners' suppers and call in for the odd cuppa throughout the night.

19

Cooking tonight

I was now rapidly approaching the final few months until my release. I was becoming quite 'demob happy' and with the excitement of it all my alcoholic intake was getting out of control, I was getting drunk most nights.

On one particular night I was disturbed by a smashing of glass coming from the dining hall. I hid in the kitchen area, waiting to see what it might have been, then suddenly I saw a shadowy figure drunkenly lurching around the kitchen trying to see what he could steal to eat. In the darkness of the kitchen I couldn't see who he was. Suddenly he passed a shaft of light coming from the office; it was the little shit who was the food grabber at the serving hatch. I let out an almighty roar that frightened me, let alone him, and smashed him in the mush so hard it knocked him out. The rage I was in was so intense (alcohol-induced), that I began to shove him in the red hot oven. 'Burn you bastard, burn,' I was repeating over and over again. I hated the little shit. Suddenly I was grabbed from behind and saw it was the RPs, coming in for their cuppas,

'What you doing, Coggee?' one asked.

'Burning the bastard,' I replied.

I explained that I had heard someone breaking in, said that I was attacked from behind and that as we struggled we fell on to the open oven door and that I was pulling him up, and he was so pissed he didn't even know where he was.

They took him back to the guardhouse, he was charged with breaking and entering the cookhouse and assaulting the Cook Corporal (me) and pleaded guilty, due to his drunken state, claiming he couldn't remember a thing. I don't doubt that: after the clout I gave him, I don't think an elephant would remember. Anyway he got 14 days' jankers and a near-death experience in the oven. I just thank God that those RPs came in when they did, otherwise I would have been in for a right roasting (pun).

I didn't have it all my own way, however. I remember when there was another break-in; he was another flash git who had probably heard of my previous exploits with his mate and the oven. I wasn't aware of him creeping up on me, not until I felt a terrific blow to the back of my head. Talk about stars in your eyes. I was knocked to the floor and he sat astride me raining blows to my head and face but he couldn't knock me out even though I wished he would – but I never succumbed to his brutal beating.

'You f***ing no good bastard, I will kill you next time I see you,' I mumbled between bloody lips and rapidly closing black and cut eyes.

Realizing he couldn't do any more, he got off my prone body and legged it out of the cook house. I was glad I only had about six weeks to do now, as I felt that there was an anti-Cockney bias sentiment which was emanating from the oven incident. There was another occasion when I was sure that this was the case.

One night, after going for my regular night at the NAAFI, I returned to the cookhouse to prepare the breakfast. I had to go into the refrigerator to get the bacon out. I thought I heard a noise outside the fridge and turned to see if anyone was there, when suddenly the door was slammed shut. When the door of a fridge is shut the light goes out – and there isn't a handle to open it.

The horror of Wales was back with me again, claustrophobia, the blackness of the coal cellar, the fear of being locked in, I was literally screaming to be let out, banging on the door until my knuckles were covered in blood. I eventually collapsed, physically and emotionally spent. How long I was in the fridge, I don't know, but suddenly I heard the click of the door being opened, followed by the sound of running footsteps. By the time I had struggled to my feet, I was in no state to chase anyone. Revenge was all I could think of, I was obsessed by it.

I began to have an idea who the culprit was: the lad who couldn't knock me out. He began to give out little hints like 'Got a cold yet, Ed?' or 'Wearing your winter woolies yet?' I let his taunts go by, as I had no doubt my revenge would not be long coming now.

20

A Cook's Revenge is Sweet

I had only one week to go now and then I would be back with my lovely Lena. I had been instructed to train up another cook to take my place when I left, and this would give me time to plan my revenge. I knew he visited the NAAFI every night and walked back with his mate, and then after his mate left him, he walked on alone to his billet.

On the night I waited outside the NAAFI for him, as he came out I saw that he was alone, which was handy. I kept to the shadows, well disguised with my balaclava and gloves on, and saw he was the worse for drink. When he approached an unlit area I caught him by surprise. I smashed a bottle over his head which broke, knocking him out cold, and I then stabbed him in the throat with it. The no good f***ing bastard had deserved all he had got; locking me in that fridge had brought back all my Welsh nightmares.

The lad was taken to the military hospital where he was treated for a very bad throat injury. The bastard should have died for causing me such anguish; however he wouldn't be any more trouble to me, I would be long gone before he left hospital.

I had heard that the SIB (Special Investigation Branch) was carrying out an investigation into finding out who had attacked the lad, as he said he had no idea who it was. I think he knew it was me, but also knew he would end up in the glass house with me, as he had initiated the first attack on me in the cookhouse and was responsible for locking me in the fridge.

Demob day, at last. We were given our discharge books and told the reserve units we would be going to, which we would have to report to as soon as we docked in the UK.

21

There's a Spy in My Soup

Below I enclose the details of my discharge papers.

Name E.L. Cogger. Rank Cpl
Army no. 23018587.
T A unit. 121 a.p.I.s. (Aerial Photographic Intelligence Service)
(Intelligence Corps, T A)

2 Borers Passage
Cutler St
London E.1.

Remarks: Cpl Cogger has been employed as a BII Cook. He is willing and hard working and is well able to take responsibility. He is clean and thoroughly honest and has a pleasant disposition.

Military Conduct. Very Good.

I don't recognise that bloke. That was all because they thought I was poor Nobby Clark, a regular soldier. Still, it wasn't his fault my scones didn't rise.

When I reported to Borers Passage, Cutler Street, I was expecting one of those TA (Territorial Army) centres, but was surprised to find it was just a door with a highly polished brass plate on the door. I pressed the doorbell and the door was opened by a replica of Regimental Sergeant Major Britain: he was tall, upright, buckles polished to the highest standard, boots like mirrors. He was a military policeman. He asked who I was and what I wanted. I showed him all the information I had and he told me to wait whilst he went into a office, returning and indicating for me to follow him leading me into a room. There was an officer sitting at a desk. The Sergeant told me to stand to attention and, as they do, bellowed, 'Corporal Cogger, sir.'

The officer outlined who they were and what they did. They were, as I gathered, an intelligence corps which deciphered aerial photographs gathered over enemy lines and I was the Cook Corporal, not a spy – what a shame. I never heard a word from them again.

When I got home, I threw all of my Army kit and uniform away, 'Bollocks to the lot of you,' I said, and went to see my beautiful Lena.

22

Back Home

I had been home for a few weeks now, my lovely Lena was now 19 and had matured into a really glamorous young woman, and the little girl I had first met had gone. The little playful cygnet had now developed into a beautiful swan. I proposed to her at the end of April 1956 and I was overwhelmed when she accepted. We decided to get married on 27th September 1956. Lena and I got officially engaged in June and set our sights on earning as much as possible for our wedding.

I had got myself a job with a firm called Trenthams, working behind the cement mixer at the Briggs Motor Company where we were building a vast new body plant (which was eventually sold to Ford Motor Company). My mate who worked with me behind the mixer was a giant of a man, well over 6 feet tall, and weighed in at about 35 stone. Everyone in Dagenham knew him, he was called Fat Olly. When he got on a bus it used to dip down about 12 inches. I was lucky to have him with me behind the mixer, as he had enormous hands and he was able to fill his shovel with twice the amount I was capable of. It was very lucky as we were on a bonus and it came in very handy to go towards our wedding savings. I did seven days a week on that job. Unfortunately it was rumoured that Olly would not live very long due to his being overweight and a genetic effect he suffered from.

Lena also worked very hard, at the Ever Ready Battery Factory in Dagenham.

23

Wedding Bells

Our wedding was fast approaching. Lena had chosen to have a rainbow wedding with seven bridesmaids, wearing gowns representing the seven colours of the rainbow. Lena's mum worked for months machining all the bridesmaids' dresses and her dad, although in very poor health, managed to save up towards his daughter's wedding for which we are eternally grateful. Sadly they are no longer with us, God bless them both. Lena's brother Bennie was to be my best man.

On the eve of the wedding some of the bridesmaids were staying over. All of the bridesmaids were Lena's cousins except my baby sister, Tina, who was now two years old. I was making myself useful putting the final bits together. The girls were all laughing and joking together, making innuendos and such about the wedding night. Lena, being a shy girl, was giggling and laughing uncontrollably at some of their remarks, until through nervousness she farted, the first time she had done this in my presence. It wasn't to be the last in the following 50-odd years though.

I got up early on the morning of our wedding to have a bath. I wanted to pump the water up while it was boiling. In those days we had a gas copper, a removable tube and a pump with which you would pump the boiling hot water upstairs into the bath. You would then have to fill up the copper with cold water again. As there were five of us, I didn't want to wait for the water to get hot again and go through all that rigmarole.

My first port of call was the second most important thing of the day, a visit to Morrie's the barbers. They all knew in the shop that I was getting married that day and Morrie said, 'Eddie, my boy, today I will give you the best DA and Pashana shampoo ever, as my wedding present to you', and he did. I didn't give a f**k if I smelt like the biggest queer in town, today I was going to marry the most beautiful girl in the world.

I had agreed to meet Bennie and all the male guests at the Cross Keys Pub which was opposite the church Lena and I were getting married in. However, I met Bennie on the corner of the notorious Church Elm Pub; we didn't want to go in there now as that was the haunt of my mates, the Heathway Gang. Bennie and I walked to the church – no car for the bridegroom and best man in those days, all right if you had a few bob to splash out, otherwise it was 'shank's pony' (on foot).

We eventually arrived at the Cross Keys Pub; we looked in and saw that most of the guests had arrived. Someone bought us a pint, joking, 'You'll need more than that tonight, my son, to keep your strength up, especially the old pecker', to guffaws of laughter.

The time had arrived for me to go and receive my bride at the altar; we had heard that the cars fetching my darling Lena and the bridesmaids had left the house and were on their way. We made our way across the road to the church and took our places, Bennie at my side. We were

Our wedding day.

94

both immaculately dressed in light gray full-length drape suits, 14-inch bottoms and white spivvy socks. Ben was a really handsome young man, and like his sister he had beautiful blond hair.

Waiting for her to arrive seemed like forever, but in actuality it was probably minutes. My mouth was dry and I began to tremble uncontrollably, until suddenly the organ struck up with the 'Wedding March'. I nervously glanced around and there she stood, with her father, the rays of the sun creating a shimmering kaleidoscope of colour reflecting through the tiara sitting upon her beautiful blonde hair. The pure white veil and wedding dress reached down to her satin shoes; in her hands she held a bouquet of deep red roses. She looked a glimmering mirage of beauty as she came down the aisle towards me.

The seven bridesmaids looked absolutely stunning in their rainbow dresses. Just as the ceremony was starting I heard a child start to cry, then start screaming. The vicar stopped in mid-sentence, and looking round I saw it was my baby sister. My mum had no alternative but to take her out of the church so my dear mum never saw me wed my lovely little Lena.

24

The Wedding Party

We arrived back at Lena's house, which I would now be living in. The house was three up, one down, with a kitchen adjoining the living room, so with all the guests, my aunts and uncles who lived in Manor Park, in the East End of London, and Lena's family from Canning Town, it was quite a squeeze. Luckily it was a sunny day so the overspill was able to go into the garden.

Everything was going swimmingly as the evening was drawing in. We had to go up to the off licence to get some more quarts of brown and light ales and some more gin and tonic.

'F**k me Ben, I didn't think they would get through all that f***king lot, you got anything left in the kitty?' I asked.

'No,' he replied, 'we'll have to have a whip-round, if we need any more.'

'Greedy bastards,' I said.

When we got back everyone was really having a good laugh as Queenie (Lena's mum) was singing her party piece, 'The Laughing Policeman'. She was quite a plump woman and when she got to the laughing bit her whole body wobbled, and had us all in stitches. My dad gave us his rendition of 'Hear My Song, Violetta' and my mum sang 'Sally'.

My mum was a really beautiful woman, and she was only 40 when Lena and I got married; my dad was the same age. Unfortunately both of them were terribly jealous of each other and although they loved each other deeply, when they were in drink they fought each other like cat and dog. I think that's what made me a vicious person at times, that and the evacuation thing and the war time experiences I had to endure. It wasn't long before it all kicked off: my dad thought one of Lena's uncles was paying too much attention to my mum.

'Take your bleeding eyes off of her,' he shouted at him, 'or you'll get a smack on the f***ing nose.'

'Who do you think you're f***ing talking to you short arsed little bastard?' replied Lena's Uncle Jim.

That set it all off: mayhem exploded, Dad stuck a right-hander on Uncle Jim, and Uncle Mick – one of the most feared men in the East End, pre the Kray twins era – hit my old man a mighty blow, knocking him senseless; he was nearly there anyway, with drink. In the end it was like a scene from one of those cowboy films, everyone fighting everyone else, chairs being thrown, tables overturned, wives trying to sort out who was who amongst the writhing mass of bodies.

Eventually calm was restored. My old man, having recovered from his enforced kip and not knowing about all the trouble he had caused, asked, 'Is there any beer left?'

While all this mayhem was going on Lena's dad, a lovely man, sat in the kitchen as he suffered from emphysema, a serious lung condition, which made it very difficult for him to breathe. He tried to ignore what was going on in the other room; however, I remember he loved a cowboy film, and he would have loved the one going on next door.

As the night was ending I got a bit tearful with all that had happened. Mainly I was sorry for my darling bride Lena, who had to suffer the indignity of having her wedding ruined. Her family had gone home and my family was still hanging about, looking for more booze. In the end

Bennie – my Best Man.

I flipped my lid and dramatically ran into the bathroom and locked myself in. What for I don't know, but it definitely wasn't to have a crap.

After a while someone noticed I was missing and new brother-in-law Bennie, who was well pissed himself, tried the bathroom door and found it was locked. He and a couple of my mates, Jerry the black boy and Ginger Walford, broke the door down. On hearing them start to break the door in, I opened the window of the downstairs toilet and jumped out. I ran over to the allotment that Lena's dad rented and sat down on a bench and cried my eyes out. Meanwhile Bennie, seeing the toilet empty, shouted hysterically 'He's jumped out of the window', over and over, until he collapsed and had some sort of fit. Lena was panicking as she thought it was an upstairs window. However she was relieved that there wasn't a body lying there – and so was I.

At last it was all over. It had gone two o'clock in the morning and Queenie said we should leave all the mess until the morning, which I was grateful for, obviously.

In those days it was rare for working people to have honeymoons. One normally got married on a Saturday, sometimes had Sunday off, and normally lived with the mother-in-law. You then put your name on the council's waiting list for a council flat or house and waited for two or three years, or had a child and got points which would further your chance of getting at least a flat.

25

Honeymoon in a 3-foot-wide Bed

At last my little Lena and I would be able to consummate our wedding, the final act of true love we had for each other. Well, that's how it's supposed to be, but Lena was more of a child bride, innocent, nervous, naive and probably imagining I was Heathcliff to her Kathy in *Wuthering Heights*. She even asked if I would turn the light off while we undressed.

Our bed, which was her bed, was just 3 feet wide. The only other thing that was in her room was a little food larder about 18 inches long by 1 foot high, which held some tea, sugar, biscuits and milk. It also only had one door; the other one was missing. This was our honeymoon suite, a 3-foot-wide bed and a small larder with one door missing.

When I finally managed to clamber over her, with all my bits and pieces dangling over her – as she had insisted that she always slept on the outside of the bed – I began to think of that Peter Sellers and Mia Zetterling film where he was trying to get his oats and he couldn't get his flies undone. I burst into fits of laughter thinking of that, Lena thought I was laughing at her but when I explained it to her, she relaxed and we settled down. She was astonished that, as she put it, I had a 'furry bum'. I smiled to myself at her innocence and we made the most wonderful love to each other. Well, the bed being only 3 feet wide we couldn't miss.

During the night I was awoken by a rustling sound, and I awoke Lena.

'Can you hear that noise?' I said. She was half asleep; I suppose she thought I was after some more loving. I said again, 'What's that noise?'

'I don't know,' she replied. 'It's probably the wind blowing the leaves about, go back to sleep.'

I tried to get back to sleep but it was no good. I woke Lena up again. 'I'm going to put the light on, Lena,' I said, leaping off the bed and switching on the light, forgetting that my darling wife was seeing me in the nude for the first time.

She screamed her head off.

'What's the matter?' I asked.

'Behind you!' she cried. 'Behind you.' Now I know that I have a hairy bum – not a furry one as she described it – but she was overdoing it a bit. 'Look behind you in the larder!' cried Lena.

I did and it was furry: about six of them, mice, and the little bastards were eating my little Lena's honeymoon breakfast. Well, with all our modesty now unashamedly exposed, I with my dingle dangling and Lena with her beautiful firm naked body, we set about the mice with whatever came to hand. Unfortunately they disappeared where they came from, under the skirting board.

On that night 50 years ago Lena made a remark to me which I don't know if she was serious about or not, she said, 'We were lucky that only one door was missing otherwise they would have all got in!'

She was so naive that she didn't even know where babies came from. Well, about three months after we got married, she would soon find out, as she was six weeks pregnant. My brother Alec's wife Jean had just had her first baby; she would give her all the info. It probably frightened the life out of her when she found out.

26

Weekend Honeymoon Over

After our weekend honeymoon it was back to the grind, and I was back behind the cement mixer with Fat Olly. Lena used to wait for me on the doorstep to come home from work and would see me and Olly coming down the road and would say 'You two look just like Laurel and Hardy.' God bless you, Olly.

The work at Briggs eventually came to an end and I then got a job on the new Ford Engine Plant which was being started next to the Briggs Body Plant. My job was with the piling gang which involved a concrete pile being driven about 30 feet into the ground. I would use a pneumatic drill to expose the reinforcing bars at the top of the concrete pile, leaving a 3-inch exposed piece of rod. The rods were about half an inch round and thousands of these piles were driven into the ground.

I was working in the piling gang one day when suddenly a dumper truck got too near the edge of one of the trenches and the driver took avoidance action, forcing me to overbalance. I could see that I was going to land on the rods and I was unable to do anything about it. The pain I had when my foot landed on the spikes of the rods was indescribable. They had gone through the bottom of my foot and come out through the top. When the ambulance came for me, I don't know how they lifted my foot off the spikes, but I bet that little bastard who I had put in the oven, would be laughing his f***ing head off, if he could see me now. What goes around comes around, as they say.

At the hospital I was taken to, East Ham Memorial, they treated me for the injuries I had suffered, gave me several injections including penicillin, bandaged my foot, gave me some crutches and sent me on my way. Lena was most surprised when I hobbled in and explained what had happened to me. I spared her all the gory details, as she only had about six weeks to go until she had the baby.

Unfortunately, about three days later I began to feel unwell as my foot began to throb agonizingly, and I was taken back to hospital where it was found my foot had become badly infected and there was a danger that I might have to have my foot off. My penicillin injections were increased to two a day and an ambulance was sent to pick me up twice a day to have the injections administered at the hospital.

A couple of nights later the pain was intense and I began to itch terribly. Lena took off the bed clothes as I was sweating profusely; as she did she gave a little cry, 'Ed, your body's covered in big red blotches.'

Her dad said, 'I don't like the look of that, best call an ambulance.' Looking down at my body I thought, f***ing hell I look like a bleeding alien. At the hospital it was ascertained that I had developed penicillin poisoning and I was given an antidote. They found out I was allergic to penicillin and I was put on another antibiotic. Eventually I recovered.

My worry now was my Lena, as she only had a couple of weeks to go now. Lena's mum and dad had put in for a larger council house when they found out that she was expecting, as we would need an extra living room. As her dad had this terrible lung disease, the council would put them on top of the list, on health grounds. Within a week of being put on the Council Transfer List, they had an offer of a two down, three bedroom house at Five Elms in Dagenham, which they had no hesitation in accepting. We got stuck in and arranged for the removal van to arrive.

The following day Lena was taken into hospital and about six hours later she soon, very painfully, found out where babies came from – and it wasn't a stork, well not the flying type! 'Stalk' is Cockney for the male fertilizing organ: 'stamen' according to the *Oxford Dictionary*, or 'hard-on' also defined in the OD. Well, we all talked of 'having the stalk' when we were sexually aroused.

Within a fortnight I was at the hospital to take home my newborn son and my darling Lena to our new home. She had left her old home and was now bringing her own son into a new one. He was a beautiful little boy and we named him Edward (Eddie) after me. He weighed in at 8 pounds and 7 ounces, a future Middleweight in the making.

I didn't go back to work at the Ford Plant again.

There were two massive projects to be started; one was the West Thurrock Power Station which was looking to employ two thousand men. I had applied for employment at the West Thurrock site and was taken on as a rigger and steel erector.

My dad had really been struggling with his bookmakers business. I couldn't see him going on much longer. He was now in dire straits, as unfortunately for him the Government had now legalised betting, and

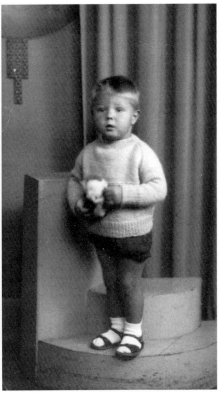

She said I was Heathcliff to her Kathy.
We had our first son, who was six weeks
old when we had this photo taken.

Eddie Junior.
Approximately three years of age.

betting shops were now springing up all over the country. My poor old man never had the finances to carry on and had to look for a job. Under rules negotiated by the trade unions, employers had to take on a certain amount of disabled workers; my dad was taken on at the West Thurrock site as a tea boy. He had fallen from the dizzy heights of being one of the wealthiest men in Dagenham to a tea boy, but there was one advantage to this. With all the men going to be employed on this project they would need a bookies' runner, who better than a disabled tea boy! My dad started on the site before me and was still there when I left.

The firm I worked for was called Babcock & Wilcox. The steel structure had already been erected; it was basically a empty shell about 400 feet high, with an enormous submarine-shaped boiler at the top of the structure from which my gang would be fixing the pipes to the places where they had to be positioned ready to be welded.

Although there was some scaffolding in place, there had to be gaps to allow the pipes, which were winched 400 feet up to us to hang them on half-inch wire strops, one each end of the pipe. We used to take a hell of a risk at that height. We used to stand on the swinging pipes to tie on the pipe which was coming up from below. I was there for about two years and there were at least six fatalities – including Lena's uncle, who fell 200 feet – and there were also many critical injuries.

On the day that Lena's uncle fell, I was working at the top level, about 400 feet up, when I heard a blood-curling scream; it was obvious that someone had fallen. As the mournful wail of the siren started, we knew that someone has been badly injured or killed. When someone is killed on a site, no one knows who has been killed as the next of kin have to be informed. The normal practice is for the site to shut down, in respect for the deceased. I had no idea who had fallen, but when we went out for a drink later I bought a evening paper and as I was glancing through it, I happened to see a small write-up: 'Steel Erector Killed in 200-foot Fall at Thurrock Power Station'. They named him as Albert Samson, Lena's mum's brother. She was inconsolable, as was Lena.

I can also recall a particular incident which was terrifying for the person involved. When a power station is near completion a water pressure test is carried out to see if all the welding is complete and there are no leaks. When the tests are carried out it is very dangerous, as the massive boiler is filled up with hundreds of thousands of gallons of water. My gang and about 20 other workers were the only persons allowed on the site. The siren was then sounded to warn that testing was about to take place. When the engineers inspected the large electronic valves they found that there was a problem as the water wasn't pouring out as they had expected. Unfortunately, a worker who was on the boiler level and not aware of the valve problem, thinking that all the water had drained out of the boiler, tried to open the hatch manually but it wouldn't budge so he picked up a large scaffold pole and proceeded to hit the hatch with it. Suddenly, without warning, the hatch flew open and a huge roar came from inside the boiler, and in a split second the man was sucked towards the hatch.

What had happened was that when the man had struck the hatch with the scaffold pole, he had unknowingly broken the vacuum of pressure which had built up in the large pipes which resulted in the water being instantly released down the pipes that then sucked him to the hatch opening. When all the water had been released, easing of the suction then allowed the man to fall onto the gantry. He was a large man with a large stomach, fortunately for him, as if he had been smaller he would have been sucked right into the boiler. His clothes had all been sucked off him and he had been seriously injured. He had a massive blood blister the same shape as the boiler opening where all his blood had been sucked to his stomach.

Unfortunately I was one of the gang sent into the boiler to clean out his clothes that were sucked off him. I went in first, and we had torches, but as the last person of the gang came into the boiler and blocked out the daylight, it came back to me: the coal cupboard in Wales, the fridge in the army, claustrophobia. I panicked. 'Let me out, let me out,' I cried. There was pandemonium as they all had to back up; although the boiler was about 60 feet in circumference the actual inside is only about 3 feet.

A few months later I was made redundant and started to seek another job. Then I started a new job with Ginger Walford (one of the Heathway Gang) and my sister-in-law's brother Dennis Henderson. We were employed as sheeters, and although the other two were experienced, I wasn't.

The first job I went with them to was in the Royal Albert Docks. I have never worked so hard or been so scared in my life. In those days we had to hump the asbestos sheets about 30 feet up a ladder. The sheets were about 6 feet wide by 8 feet long. You then balanced the sheet by holding the bottom width of the sheet with your right hand then, resting the sheet on your head and shoulder, climbed up the ladder and placed it in position on the purlin – with nothing to save you if you fell. You then had to do what they called ducking, that is, place your left leg and arm on the top of the sheet and duck under the sheet and, hanging upside down, you stretched your right arm as far as you could to push a bolt which hooked under the purlin through a hole that had been drilled by your mate, working on top of the sheet. That job took months and I shat myself every day worrying if it would be the last time I would see my lovely Lena and baby son again.

Unfortunately Dennis lost an eye when he was hit by a jagged piece of metal which flew off the edge of a chisel he was using. Then about a year later I had an accident. We were building a Customs lock-up when it suddenly collapsed, throwing me and a couple of the others about 30 feet to the ground. We were taken to hospital and I was diagnosed with a slipped disc and bruises. The back injury was quite serious and the doctors decided that I would be put in a plaster cast. It was the most embarrassing moment of my life. I believe there is a saying, that 'tiny acorns grow into great oak trees'; well that's a load of bullshit.

I don't know if the procedure has changed in the last 40-odd years since I had my slipped disc, but this is how my treatment went. I was pushed into the plaster room of the hospital to be met by two female nurses and a male nurse, who did a brilliant take-off of Frankie Howerd. In fact he was more camp than the real one was. 'Hello ducky, what have you been up to?' he asked, arms flailing like Old Mother Riley. 'Does it hurt?'

I thought, that's all I f***ing want, a prick of a queer boy, asking 'does it hurt', stupid mincing bastard. Well, embarrassing as it was, this is what happened. I was already in a wheelchair; they strung a bandaged strop around my neck which was attached to a rope and pulley and Frankie Howerd began to pull the rope which then began to stretch my neck and gradually lifted me off the chair until I was on tip-toes.

Frankie then offered sympathetic mutterings: 'That didn't hurt you, did it blossom?' How the f**k does he know? It got worse. 'We'll take your gown off now, Edward,' one of the nurses said. I thought to myself oh no, not that, two possible virgins and a wigless ponce of a Frankie Howerd look-alike, were stripping me, and my acorn (what a circumcised prick looks like) was beginning to disappear in ever-decreasing inches into the lower regions of my stomach, like the Sergeant Major's ever-decreasing circles until you run up your own arse.

When I look back, all those years ago, I don't remember if the Carry On films had been made yet, but this situation I was in would have made an ideal script for *Carry on Nursing*. Here was I, strung up like a naked eunuch, swinging round and round, my 'Old Bill' rapidly disappearing to God knows where, having some bent plasterer of Paris wrapping my body in a muslin bandage. He was then going to plaster me from the top of my chest all the way down and around my body to my disappearing private parts; in fact, I would be like a walking barrel for at least six months. I was left dangling in this position until the plaster of Paris set.

I walked to the ambulance like a Frankenstein's monster and was taken home. When I got home, Lena nearly fainted.

'My God, Ed, what's happened to you?'

'Don't ask me yet, love,' I replied, trying to recall the events of the day and trying to explain them to her.

One of the problems I had was that no one at the hospital had informed me how I would be able to sit or lie down. As the plaster was sitting on two pads on my hips, going up my chest to my nipple area and armpits, obviously I couldn't hold my arms by my side, hence the Frankenstein's gait.

When I tried to go to bed, which I found impossible, we devised a system where Lena would hold my hands, stand on my feet and gently lower me onto the bed, and then swing my whole body around so that I was in the correct position. I was so pleased that when I lay on the bed, the plaster would rise a bit enabling me to look down inside the plaster and see my Old Bill had returned to normal, Frankie Howerd would have been pleased, anyway.

After about two weeks I was getting somewhat bored with lying about. By this time, I had mastered the art of 'roll out the barrel', which entailed me rolling onto my stomach and pulling myself up with my arms with whatever was available, usually Lena. I was also missing my Sunday pint with the lads at the Cherry Tree pub which was our local, so I decided to venture out and try to walk the mile to the pub.

I decided to ponce myself up like most of the gang would. The drape suite, white shirt and flashy tie, suede 3-inch brothel creepers, my prized 'guards-back' overcoat, and to top it all, a Stetson (which I had nicked on a previous occasion from a local nightclub), which was perched upon my over-lacquered duck's arse hair.

I knew who was there at the time the hat was nicked and know that two of them are definitely not with us any more (Ronnie and Reggie Kray) but I guess there might be one or two golden oldies still about.

It wasn't a very nice day to take a chance walking to the pub. There was quite a bit of ice about and a strong wind gusting, but I was keen to show off my plaster waistcoat. So onward I went, slowly but surely, arms out, looking like a baddie gunslinger from a B movie, I strode on, carefully picking my way through the ice which gradually began to look like icebergs the further I went.

I was about half way to the pub when it started to snow. F**k it, I said to myself, I've made a right cock-up here. It began to snow quite heavily now and the wind was becoming stronger, my appearance had now changed from a gunslinger to a snowman as the plaster cast was making me look more rotund.

Inevitably it happened: I stood on a ridge of ice and my feet went from under me and seemed to fly above my head, my Stetson went flying down the road. I then had the problem of trying to get to my feet, without Lena's help. I rolled all over the pavement and off it trying to get up; if a car had come along then, the driver would have mistaken me for a snow-covered speed bump. With the help of some local evergreens I eventually pulled myself up into some sort of standing position although the plaster cast had, with all the struggling and twisting and turning I had done, somehow twisted around and the two pads were no longer sitting on my hips as they were normally, but one was being held up by my now back to normal cock and the other one was sliding down the crease of my arse.

I finally arrived at the Cherry Tree, now looking like Worzel Gummidge, my eyes staring as though I was suffering from snow blindness, my lacquered hair standing on end as though I had just seen the Abominable Snowman. And as if to take the piss, the governor shouted out, 'Time, gentlemen, please.' Bastard.

I had to wear the plaster for about four months and then was measured for a body brace, which was much more comfortable although I still wasn't able to bend my back.

27

Mad House

My brother Alec was now out of the Army, having served about two and a half years instead of the two years he should have done, due to being absent without leave so much. In the end they used to regularly send an Army ambulance complete with a big red cross, and a doctor to examine him to see if he was fit for duty. There were a few doctors about in those days who would take a back-hander to sign a sick note. That's why they sent an Army doctor to examine the patient – especially my brother as he was the star of the boxing team.

Anyway some friends of my dad, four brothers named Lambert, ran a chimney sweeping business in Upton Park and my brother worked for them. They were all ex-boxers and took a great interest in my brother's career. I asked my brother if he would ask them if they had any jobs going. I was well pleased to hear that they would be starting work on a project soon and I would be ideal, as they knew I could only do light work, as I was still on the sick list at Babcock & Wilcox.

The day soon came round and I was looking forward to working again. My brother had put me in the picture as to what I would be doing: he explained that we were going to a hospital to clean the chimneys. My job would be to receive the pipe from each of the hospital wards' windows as it was lowered down to me and attach it to the industrial vacuum cleaner that I would be operating on the ground.

That's all I had to do, he said: 'Just press the green button to start, the red to stop, OK?' 'Easy,' I replied.

We arrived at the hospital to find the gates were closed. As I was sitting in the back of the van with my brother I asked what the hold-up was but he didn't know, so I poked my head around the side of the van and saw a very large notice which read:

BARLEY LANE MENTAL HOSPITAL
VISITORS AND WORKMEN SHOULD BE AWARE THAT
SOME PATIENTS ARE UNPREDICTABLE

F***ing Hell. That's another fine mess you've got me into, Stanley!

The gates were opened by a stroppy gateman wanting to know the ins and outs of a duck's arse; he could see who we were by the sign on the van: 'Lamberts Chimney Sweep'. Mind you, he might have had some justification when he looked in the back and saw my brother and I, because with all the soot that had blown about as we were driving to the hospital we now looked like a couple of Kentucky minstrels.

We were eventually allowed in and set about setting all the equipment up. The pipe was lowered down to me and as instructed, I pressed the green button to start the vacuum cleaner. As soon as the engine started up pandemonium set in, as patients from the wards came charging towards me, evidently because this contraption was making the unruliest noise imaginable. I shouted up to the open windows above me, asking the others to come down and give me some support. I didn't know what the reaction of the inmates would be as I had never been in a *One Flew Over The Cuckoo's Nest* situation before. (Obviously this film had not been made then, but my memory and imagination lead me to believe that's what it would have been like.)

Anyway I wasn't surprised when a Jack Nicholson-type character came up to me and asked what I was doing. I replied that I was cleaning the chimneys. 'How?' he asked. I didn't want to get into a how and why situation with him, so I just explained to him what I was doing: green button on, red button off. There was quite a gathering around me now. One elderly lady was asking me if I knew where her daughter was and why she wasn't coming to see her, others were asking if I had any fags. As I was facing a barrage of questioning about this and that, I saw Jack Nicholson f***ing about with the buttons. 'Green on, red off', he kept repeating to himself. Shit, he had got the hang of it quicker than I had.

I then got into a 'quickest finger on the button' situation with J.N. – me on, him off. Meanwhile up in the wards they were wondering what was going on. 'What the f**k's going on down there?' called one of them. I didn't recognise who it was, as their faces were so sooty they looked more like the singing group The Ink Spots, rather than my brother and the Lambert brothers.

In the end we got the hospital to ensure a male nurse supervised the wards we were sweeping and eventually he ended up being the green on, red off man – for a bung, mind you – allowing me to go to the wards to assist the others. I then learned the trade of chimney sweeping. It took two minutes. It always amused me when the inmates, who by now had learned the routine, waited expectantly for the brush to pop out of the chimney pot. I would always know when that had happened as a big cheer would arise from below.

After a while I had to pack the job in. My father-in-law's emphysema was getting quite serious and the smell of the soot was affecting him. So it was back to the norm (well, if you could call it that).

I had taken advice from my trade union's solicitors regarding my accident and was told that I had a very good claim against my employers and that they would represent me, which I was well chuffed with.

28

Mad House (Part 2)

As you might have come to conclude, our household was not quite as normal as others would be: ours was a very dysfunctional and violent family. My dad, maybe because of his 60-foot fall and the terrific injuries he suffered, or his upbringing (I understand that his father had a terrible temper), was to blame. It's in the genes.

My younger brother Alec had recently got married to his wife Jean. He had met her when he was a barrow boy, selling cherries. She was still at school when he first met her. I don't know what his chat-up line was: 'Would you like a cherry?' I guess. Jean is a real laugh so I can only imagine she would have had a saucy answer in reply. They lived with our nan and granddad in Manor Park, East London. This was ideal for Alec as this was closer to his work at the Lamberts. They lived there for a while but Jean became pregnant, so about two months before the baby was born they moved into my parents' house in Valence Circus, Dagenham.

One night after having had a good piss-up round the Cherry Tree, for some reason or another an almighty row broke out between Alec and my old man. When my old man got drunk he used to act very theatrically. He would stretch his braces at arm's length above his head, bend over with them still over his head, go into a rant and rave, stand up straight again and let go of his braces which would twang like a catapult. I half expected to see him propel himself into space one day. Mum must have sewn on his buttons with twine.

Well, a fight broke out between them and as Alec was a brilliant boxer he soon put the old man down and, having had enough of his ranting, he went to the room he and Jean lived in. Jean was already in bed and she asked Alec what the row was about. As he was about to tell her, Dad rushed into the room with a carving knife in his hand. He attempted to stab Alec, who ducked and Dad fell on top of Jean who was in her nightclothes, scrambling to get out of the way. Alec went to help her and as he did so, Dad stabbed him in the thigh.

An ambulance was called, and took them away, Alec on one stretcher, Jean on the other. He had his leg stitched. All the excitement had brought Jean into labour and she had a lovely baby boy, who came out fighting!

Alec and Jean had decided that my parents' house wasn't exactly the right atmosphere to bring up a newborn baby, so they applied to Basildon New Town Council for a council house. The conditions for getting a house were, that you had to be employed in Basildon which, being a new town, was seeking workers of all kinds (craftsmen, labourers, shop workers etc). Obviously they had to house all these workers, so Alec applied for a job and was successful. Within a month they had moved into a beautiful new council house.

This left just my younger brother now living at home with my parents. He was just about 17 but again, like Alec, had become a brilliant boxer. He was picked to fight for the London Team against the Moscow Team and won in a very hard and close fight. He, like all of us, were what you would call f***ing nutters.

I recall on one occasion (well I can't forget it really) when we had been round the Cherry Tree, there was the old man, Mum, Lena, Barry and his girlfriend Pat. We were all well pissed (except for the girls) when we left the Cherry Tree. Barry and I had started arguing as we walked home; it was only about a five-minute walk from the pub, as my parents lived just behind the pub. Well, when we got in the house it all went off: he swung a punch at me I swung one back, we wrestled backwards and forwards in the scullery then into the living-room, the girls and my mum trying to separate us, the old man doing one of his Houdini acts with his braces. 'What the f**k's going on with this family?' he ranted, as we four struggled in and out of the scullery via the living room. Eventually we were separated, Lena dragging me into the living room and Pat taking Barry into the scullery.

At that point I thought it was all over but Barry was having none of it. All of a sudden a saucepan came flying into the room, hitting Lena on the head. 'You little bastard!' I shouted, and looked around for some ammunition to retaliate with. All I could see were his prized boxing trophies. I threw one at him and missed, he came back with a frying pan, I returned with another of his trophies. As I turned around to get some more ammo, Lena screamed, 'Look out Ed, he's got a knife.'

He stabbed me in the back. It went in very deep, just below my right shoulder blade, and the blood was pumping out like a small fountain. I suddenly went very weak at the knees and collapsed onto the floor.

Brother Barry (on my right) stabbed me.

Lena started screaming 'My Eddie, you've killed him!'

Pat said in a very staid manner, 'Now look what you've done, Bal.'

The old man had stopped his Houdini act in mid-action, his trousers were now around his ankles, his long johns a shade of yellow more than white.

Lena was screaming 'Get an ambulance, get the police!'

Dad was adamant. 'We don't want no police round here.'

And there was I, f***ing bleeding to death. Mum was rushing about in a flap, tidying things up in case an ambulance was called, as they do. As she was sodding about, she threw a pair of her knickers over my head; why, I don't know.

Lena started screaming again, 'He's dead, he's dead.' Much to my dad's consternation Lena said she was going to phone the police and the ambulance service. She ran to the corner phone box and dialled 999. She started calling 'Help, help!' but unfortunately some prick had cut the phone cord.

My dad was very reluctant to get the police involved or call for an ambulance, so as drunk as he was (although there weren't any drinking and driving laws in those days), he was persuaded to take me to a local doctor's surgery, who we knew would take a bung. This was about one o'clock in the morning. We rang his bell continually until an upstairs window opened.

'Vat do you vant?' an unseen voice asked.

'We want to see the doctor,' Lena said. 'My husband has fallen on some glass and is bleeding badly.'

'Take him to the hospital,' said the voice.

'We can't,' replied Lena. 'He is losing so much blood.'

'Vait a moment,' the voice replied. 'I vill come down.'

Eventually the door opened and we were ushered in. Mum was still pressing her blood-soaked knickers against my wound; she must have learned that during the war.

On examining me the doctor concluded, 'This is a stab wound' and with much head-shaking said, 'You must go to the emergency department.'

I didn't want to get involved in all that official stuff, so I asked him if he could stitch it up for me. 'No can do, no can do,' he replied. I offered him 20 quid (a lot of money in those days), and he put eight, very painful (with no painkiller) stitches in my wound. No 'hypocrite' oath when it comes to a few bob in the bin, 20 quid – what a stitch-up!

29

Two Tea Boys

As I have previously mentioned, two new power stations were to be built, one which was near completion at West Thurrock, and another one which had just started at Tilbury, both in Essex. As I said, my dad had been taken on as a tea boy some time earlier and because I was now classed as disabled due to my spinal injury, I was taken on as his deputy. 'Makes yer larf, dunnit? Deputy tea boy to your old man; Cogger and son, tea boys.'

My dad now had more time to collect his bets, with me covering for him. Luckily there was a bookmaker's shop just outside the site and he had negotiated two shillings in the pound commission with the bookie to take the bets to him. I suppose there must have been about 600 men working on the site. His commission must have averaged £20 a week then. When you take into consideration that our weekly earnings were just £20 a week, he was on a good thing.

Steel erecting in those days was a very dangerous occupation. I had many friends killed and maimed including my best mate Ginger Walford who fell about 50 feet. Perhaps if he had stayed in the Merchant Navy with me, things might have turned out differently; still, that was his destiny. We could have both been blown to smithereens on that old stinking tanker: if the Good Lord had wanted a couple of Pashana-odoured, duck-arsed yobbos amongst his flock, he would have taken us then. God bless you, Ginger.

30

Our New Home

We applied to the council to be put on the housing list. The normal procedure was to state what reasons you would have for going on the council list, as there was a three- or four-year wait. We explained to them that we now had a newborn baby. We also said that due to Lena's father's very serious chest illness, it wouldn't be the right environment to bring a new baby up in. I also got my spoke in, saying I was a green card (disabled) holder and needed certain help at times. The reason for this was that you got points. To get a house or flat you had to duck and dive, even bribe, to build your points up.

After about a year of waiting we got an offer of a ground-floor corner flat which was absolutely beautiful. We were over the moon; it was on an estate called Heath Park Estate, Dagenham. It was a lovely flat which had heating under the tiled floor and a fully fitted kitchen; it was a dream come true. We began to prepare the move to our new home.

Unfortunately we realised we didn't have the money to pay for a removal van, so I came up with the idea of asking Lambert the chimney sweep if he could move us in his van, which he agreed to do. On the morning of the move Lambert had to do a couple of chimneys on the way to us. I was a bit choked at this as the van was sooty and he also had a couple of bags of soot in it as well. Still, beggars can't be choosers as they say. It was quite a big van, but we didn't have a lot of furniture. The one-door food cabinet about which Lena said on our wedding night that we were lucky only half the mice could get in (I'm still bemused by that), had long gone.

We loaded up the van with what we had and prepared to go. Lambert asked the way to the flat. I had intended to go in the back of the van but Lena didn't know the way to the flat, so she had to ride in the back. Although everything was tied to the sides of the van, I said to Lena to be careful as the van would be swaying as we went round the corner. It would only take about ten minutes to get to the flat I said to her. Above the sound of the engine and the clatter and clanging of what we had in the back there wasn't much I could do now as we were nearly there.

When we got to the flat, I quickly jumped out of the van, opened the back doors of the van and nearly shit a brick at what I saw. It was Lena, her bleached blonde hair, which was always immaculate, now as black as soot, which was what it was. Her hands and face were as black as the ace of spades, except for her eyes which for some reason were like pissholes in the snow. She must have kept them closed when, as I later learnt, the van turned a corner rather sharply, she overbalanced and fell head first into a bag of soot.

We now started to furnish our lovely new apartment. In those days most people got their fixtures and furnishing on the never-never.

Lena was well known in the locality for her beauty, her hairstyles, and above all her eccentricity. She could make costume jewellery look like it was worth a fortune. She and her sister-in-law Jean were of the same mould, always enjoyed life to the full. Although now in their seventies they still have the same hair styles, Jean red, Lena blonde. It would be rude of me to remark on how they've stayed that colour, but there isn't a gray hair in sight! Lena's eccentricity was made obvious when we went on our first shopping trip to look for furniture for our new home.

We were looking around when Lena stopped. 'I do love that, Ed,' she remarked. I looked at what she was pointing at, it was a lavender three-piece suite, covered in vinyl. It was pointless to say no to her, as I knew she would always get her own way, especially if there was a promise on offer. There was a lavender vinyl-panelled cocktail bar, two lavender vinyl-covered padded cocktail stools, a double bed with a lavender vinyl-covered padded headboard and two single beds with lavender vinyl-covered padded headboards. She said, 'I do love lavender.' That was obvious, especially when she then had the f***ing poodle dyed lavender. She was usually known as the lady with the little white poodle, except when she changed her hair colour, and then he would be known as the little pink poodle.

Heath Park was a very nice area of Dagenham to live in; we lived in Wythenshawe Road which consisted of a mixture of flats and houses. Well, nearly everyone got on, except me and another prick who was a professional wrestler who used to wrestle on television with Jackie Pallo and Mick McManus. My heroes in those days were Bert Asseratti, Heavyweight Champion of Great Britain, and Man Mountain Dean and many others. Man Mountain Dean came into my life again later but that's another tale in my story.

As was the norm, every Friday night was men-only night. That was the night most of the Heathway Gang used to meet up at the Church Elm pub, which was on the corner of the Heathway. There would be Lennie and Harry Wiltshire, Sail Smithson, Billy Gallagher, Peter Penfold, Ginger Walford, Rabbits (Billy Thorn), Halfpenny Wilson, Billy Baker, Dougie and Billy Allsop, myself, and numerous others. Remember, this was before the Krays became prominent, they became well known when they allegedly pulled a scam, swapping places with each other when one was visiting the other in nick.

The entertainment in those days (1956) was quite bizarre; it was the time when men became female impersonators. Apparently they were in the Army and set up an entertainment company and entertained the troops wherever they were fighting. Well Trixie and the girls, as we knew them, were well capable of returning any shitty remarks we threw at them.

After turning-out time we moved outside to the jellied eel stall, ate our fill, and after f***ing about a bit, made our way home. Lennie, Harry, Ginger and I all went the same way home. They lived in the

My mum with Lena, seven months pregnant.

123

Heathway, I went about a mile further on. By the time I got home it was gone 12 o'clock.

Lena seemed somewhat upset when I got in. My lovely Lena was expecting another baby, but one wouldn't believe it, she was seven months gone but she never looked it as she still had a beautiful trim body.

'What's up, love?' I asked.

'It's that rotten git of a wrestler across the road,' she replied. 'He's had a right go at Ted.' (Ted was our upstairs neighbour.)

'Why?' I asked.

'Well, little Eddie and the wrestler's son were having a little spat as little ones do and Ted told them not to argue and play nicely. The wrestler's son went home and told the wrestler that Ted had been nasty to him. The wrestler came over to Ted and gave the poor sod a right slagging, I feel so sorry for Ted,' she replied.

'F***ing no-good bastard, I'm going over to see him.'

'No, don't go over there at this time of the night, it's gone half past 12,' she said.

I was raging. 'I'm not having a big prick like him coming over here and threatening my neighbours over my child,' I said. 'Bollocks to him.'

I went over to his house and knocked on his door. No reply. I knocked again, and after a few minutes I heard some movement and the passage light came on. The upper part of the door was made of frosted glass so that it couldn't be seen through. Suddenly the light seemed to dim as a figure covered the glass. I began to think that it must be made of magnifying glass instead of frosted; he looked much bigger close up than when he was coming home from work, as I had only seen him from a distance. Oh well, David beat Goliath. Unfortunately I didn't have a sling or a stone.

'What the f**k do you want at this time of the night?' he asked.

'I want to know why you came over to have a go at my neighbour,' I replied.

'What the f***ing hell's it got to do with you?' he said, whilst finger-jabbing me in the chest.

At the time I realised that an audience was gathering on their balconies and at their front doors. There were supporting shouts and cheers from David's supporters and, as no one liked him, boos for Goliath.

As the finger-jabbing continued I said to him, 'Do that once more and I will flatten you.'

Before I knew what was happening, I was in a Bert Asseratti bear hug, followed by a Jackie Pallo back-breaker, then a Mick McManus forearm smash and then finally he attempted a Man Mountain Dean pile-driver: that's when he would get his opponent's head in between his thighs and drop to the floor, crashing his opponent's head onto the boards.

At that moment the opponent was me, but he made a cock-up of the pile-driver as he went down; his thighs opened allowing my head to become free. As I was lighter and nimbler than him and he was struggling to get up, it gave me the opportunity to give him a right kicking in the bollocks. Over and over again I kicked him in the balls, making sure his balls were doing a disappearing act up into his groin, like he tried to drive my head into my shoulders.

It was all over then, he was lying on the ground rolling backwards and forwards clutching his bollocks and moaning in pain. David had beaten Goliath again, but I didn't half hurt.

The next day I was the people's champion. Everyone on the estate had heard about it and were unanimous that he was a bit of a pig and deserved all he got. Lennie would have been well pleased, but unfortunately he was doing another stretch. He did like a battle.

31

A New Addition to the Family

Well it was Christmas Eve 1960 at 8.45 a.m. and the milkman was delivering the milk when the midwives announced to me, dozing on the settee, that Lena had given birth to a beautiful baby boy. He weighed in at exactly 5 pounds; if he was a dog he would have been the runt of the litter. Lena already had a name picked out for him but I strongly disagreed with her.

'OK,' I said, 'What is it?'

'Tracey Reed,' she replied.

'Reed?' I said. 'Who has ever heard of someone called Reed'?

'No, you dope, Tracey, that's what I am going to call him, my little baby Tracey. It's a boy's and a girl's name.'

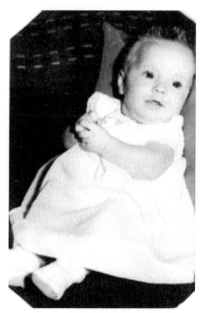

Tracey – a boy – six weeks old.

I said, 'It sounds like a right poofter's name.'

'No it's not, Ed. There's this right handsome bloke on the telly, he plays the part of a real hard-case private detective. Please, Ed, I'll do anything for you if you let me call him what I want.'

Well Lena could always twist me around her middle finger with a promise. I really couldn't give a toss what she called him anyway. Eddie our firstborn was Little Boy Blue, as she used to call him. Now she had a Tracey baby. And I had the most beautiful, innocent, scatterbrained love of my life, my lovely Lena. The milkman seemed rather pleased with the result as well.

I decided that I would go for a walk with little Eddie down to the Cherry Tree pub to break the good news to my family. They were all there, Mum, Dad, Alec, Barry, Lennie Wiltshire and a few of the boys. They were all well pleased to hear of the new baby.

When Lennie heard what Lena had called him, he cocked an eyebrow in indignation. 'Tracey? That's a f***ing bird's name, poor little bastard, tell her to change it.'

'No, straight up, Len,' I said, trying to explain Lena's private eye in the TV series, but the more I babbled on the more frustrated he got.

'Load of bollocks,' he said. I quickly changed the subject.

In the pubs those days they used to have children's rooms, where parents could go and be with their children, so my mum volunteered to go in and be with little Eddie. I had had a little 'guards-back' overcoat made for him, and she laughed when she saw him. 'You're a smart one, Eddie,' she said, as she handed him one of his favorites, an arrowroot biscuit.

Later, as we were leaving, my dad suggested that we all go round to our flat to see the new baby. I tried to dissuade them, unfortunately unsuccessfully. I didn't want to upset Lennie any more, I'd leave that to Lena.

The midwives had gone by the time we got to the flat, Lena's mum Queenie was there, she had arrived with the milky (milkman). They all piled into the bedroom, Mum 'ooing' and 'aahing', breathing stout all over our newborn. Dad similarly with his brown and mild and the others smelling of the local Romford Brewery (who later in my life would become my last employer).

By the time everyone had gone, Lena's fully stocked lavender vinyl-covered cocktail bar was empty but they all had a whip-round for the baby and Lena even talked Lennie into agreeing that Tracey was a nice name for the baby. He did insist however that we call him Trace which we do to this day.

Eddie, aged five.

Eddie as he is now.

About a year after Tracey was born, we had our first crisis in our little family unit. Eddie our eldest son was taken very ill. I was at work when I received a message to go home. When I got home, I found Lena in a terrible state. Apparently he had been watching one of the children's programmes on television. He used to lie practically underneath the television and for some reason she found him having a fit, couldn't revive him and started screaming. The next-door neighbour, who happened to be a retired nurse, knocked on the door to see if she could be of some assistance. They gave him as much help as possible until the ambulance arrived and luckily he responded to the first aid they gave him.

In the hospital, test results showed that he had a heart abnormality, a murmur. Our lovely little eldest son would have to be monitored for the rest of his life.

32

A Stranger Appears

Every Sunday we all gathered in the Cherry Tree pub in Dagenham, which was our dinner time watering hole. All the pubs in those days had their own gangs. The Heathway Gang were always associated with the Church Elm, the Cherry Tree and the Beacon.

The Chequers had the Irish (Turks, I don't know why they were called that, but the graffiti on the walls always referred to them in that way). They were immigrants from Ireland who came over to work in the newly built Ford Motor Company factory. A fight was always on the cards if you ventured into their territory.

The Merry Fiddlers was where the wrestling arena was, behind the pub. I remember when I was about 14 years of age mimicking all the moves made by all the wrestlers: Bert Asseratti's back-breaker, Rex Wheeler's flying kick, etcetera. The Merry Fiddlers and the adjacent arena were attached to a vast area of land called Nanny Goat's Common, and this was where travellers tethered their goats and horses. On this land was also an old rag and wool sorting factory owned by a huge man called Tiny Wakefield; he had two sons, Billy and Tiny Junior. They were very well known in the area. They lived in the same area that I lived in, Valence Circus. If you can imagine a hot cross bun, the circle would be the outer ring and the cross would represent the two inner roads Adamar and Aylmer. Every morning you would see them leave their house to go to their yard to saddle up the horses and carts to go totting, collecting old rags, jam jars and the like.

The Merry Fiddlers, the Travellers and the Ship, were all within 50 yards of each other. The gangs from these three pubs and the Cherry Tree and the Church Elms were basically all friends with each other.

This stranger was vaguely familiar: I hadn't seen him in the Cherry Tree before but I knew him from somewhere. He was scrutinizing the people in the pub; his piercing, unblinking, staring eyes swept around the bar, stopping briefly to look at me and then on to the rest of the boys, stopping again to look at Lennie Wiltshire.

Cassius Clay with nephew Scott when he was a young boy: One World Champion meets future World Champion.

Later, when the stranger had gone, I approached Lennie and said, 'Len there was a geezer giving you a right eyeballing earlier.'

'I know,' he replied. 'It was Roy Shaw, I know him, he's OK.'

Roy must have been about 21 then. He knew my brother Alec (Little Legs) pretty well as they had an interest in kick-boxing. My brother Alec has a photo over his mantelpiece of Cassius Clay holding my young nephew Scott Cameron when he was about three years old; he later went on to win the Junior World Kick Boxing Championship. Cassius Clay had come over to England to promote the Bruno versus Witherspoon fight in Basildon. A pitiful end to the greatest Heavyweight the world had seen.

My two brothers and I all boxed and, strangely, fought the three O'Callaghan brothers. I fought Paddy, Alec fought Johnny and Barry fought Peter. Alec won the ATC Championship of Great Britain and Barry won the London Amateur Championship. There was another brilliant boxer at our school, Roy Wingrove; I think he turned professional.

I was surprised on reading Roy Shaw's book *Hard Bastards* that Roy

Nephew Scott with trophies won when winning the World Junior Kick Boxing Championship.

hadn't mentioned Lennie Wiltshire, as I understand that he had great respect for Lennie. I saw Roy Shaw fight Lenny McLean many years ago at Cinatra's in Croydon, Surrey. An acquaintance of mine, Patsy Gutteridge, was fighting on the same bill. Teddy Onslow (Ginger Ted), who I knew quite well from the Church Elm and Thatched House pubs, was involved in the sale of the tickets.

The book *Pretty Boy, Roy Shaw* was written by Kate Kray, widow of Ronnie Kray, in 2007. I would recommend this book to anyone who has not read it. A real good read for anyone who has not seen over the other side of the fence, at the real world.

Roy Shaw and I both went into the Army in 1954 (I was two years older than him) but had been in the Merchant Navy for three years. I haven't seen 'Shawee', as we used to call him, for at least 30 years.

I have been retired over 20 years now. I was in the Thatched House, Barking for nearly 15 years and the Crown, Basildon for ten years. I believe Roy must have been away (in nick) for a lot of that time and might not recall me. I only hear of him through my brother Alec, who sees him occasionally at kick boxing shows.

I have had no contact with any of the faces I mention in my book for many years. I would love to see Lennie and Harry Wiltshire again before 'pop-off day'.

33

Return to Work

After a couple of days off work helping Lena to adjust with the new baby, I returned back to work as my old man's deputy tea boy. My stint as a make-believe chimney sweep and *One Flew Over the Cuckoo's Nest* inmate was over.

My dad was still the site's bookies runner. The bets were normally collected at the entrance to the site, placed in a clock bag and sealed in such a way that only the betting shop staff had the means of opening it. The bets had to be at the shop at least five minutes before the first race of the day.

On one particular day the collector didn't turn up. As the security guard on the gate knew me, he let me out. I rushed to the betting shop and got there just as the first race finished: I heard the name of the winner announced as I was outside the door. Never one to miss an opportunity, I quickly wrote down the name of the winner, which I can't remember now, and coupled it up with another one that I do remember (I had to take pot luck with that one, as it was in a later race) – it was the Queen's horse, Charlton.

I put the bet in the name of a regular heavy punter and rushed breathlessly into the shop asking why the clerk from the office hadn't turned up. No one seemed to know why. I just said, 'Well, here's the bets anyway,' and turned and walked out.

My old man was well pleased when I told him what I had done. He said he had better go and tell Bill (the punter) that even if the other one lost he wouldn't lose anything anyway.

At the end of the day as we queued up to get our individual work's coaches to our different destinations, the paper seller came by. '*Star Standard*,' he called out. Dad paid out his three pence and sat in his usual seat with me next to him.

'That first horse won at seven to one,' he said.

'What about the second one?' I asked.

'It's not in here,' he said.

'Look in the Stop Press,' I said. 'That's where they have the late results.'

As he was looking at the paper his cheeks suddenly puffed up like a puffer fish and as his cheeks deflated, a choking 'F***ing hell' came out of his now open mouth. He was literally gobsmacked; he couldn't speak for a while. I asked him if he was all right. 'F***ing right, I'm all right,' he said. 'The F***ing horse won at twenty to one.'

I was the one who was gobsmacked then. I worked it out roughly in my head 'That's nearly five hundred quid,' I said.

'I know,' he replied. 'Don't say a word to anyone; I have got to put Bill in the know before anyone from the betting shop gets to him.'

The following day my dad met up with Bill and explained the situation to him and told him that he would see him all right financially. Bill, who was the site convener and the biggest punter, agreed to do as my dad wanted but only if he got half of the winnings. He had my old man over a barrel; my dad had no choice but to agree.

The following day as we got on the coaches to take us to work, my dad briefed me on how I was to act when I went to the betting shop to pick up the returns. He warned me not to mention or show any reaction to the bet, as we weren't supposed to know anything about it. He emphasised, as there would obviously be something said, to act as if I hadn't a clue what they were on about.

As I approached the betting shop I composed myself as much as I could, took a deep breath and entered the shop.

'I have come for the returns for the site,' I said.

'Hang on a minute, mate,' he replied and went into the rear office. He came back saying, 'The governor wants a word with you in the office', his thumb pointing behind him.

I had never been in the office before. Here comes the third degree, I thought to myself, my imagination running away with itself. Thumbscrews next. Entering the office I saw two people, one sitting at a large desk who I presumed was the boss, the other standing arms folded, stern-faced, with a ticker tape chattering away behind him (no televisions in betting shops in those days), probably the minder.

'Would you like to tell me what happened yesterday?' he said.

With a quizzical look on my face, which I had perfected over many years (wrongly promoted in the Army, and the ducking and diving I had to do in the Merchant Navy), I asked him, 'What do you mean? In relation to what?'

'The bets, that's what I mean, the bets.'

I replied, 'No one turned up with the clock bag, so I had to run, like a two-year-old racehorse' – I was trying to bring a bit of a laugh into the situation – 'to get here in time.'

'Don't f**k with me,' he said. 'You were in here two minutes after the race was over.'

'F**k me,' I said. 'Was I that fast?' Taking the piss.

'Anyway, tell your old man to get down here and tell him all yesterday's bets are null and void.'

'Tell him your f***ing self,' I told him, giving the folded arms a good eyeballing on the way out. I fancied another bollock-kicking session with someone.

When I got back to the site and told my old man of the outcome he said he was expecting it but he said it was up to Bill the punter to do his bit now. Big Bill, as he was known on the site, was big, a good 19 stone. He was the site Union Convener and was more familiar with the law of the land than most.

As the licensing of betting shops was now legal, the bookmaker was responsible to uphold the law for himself and all his agents, which included the likes of us tea boys. It was not the fault of a tea boy if the bookmaker's agent did not turn up with a tea bag, let alone a clock bag, nor if the bookmaker then blamed the tea boy for being two minutes late and claimed he was listening at the door of the betting shop to hear the winner of the first race, writing it down, and then having the luck to pick out a 20 to one winner in a later race, just because it was the Queen's horse. Fancy someone trying to be able to rip off a bookmaker like that. It would be impossible! But I know of one who did. Meeeeeeeeeeeeee.

The bookmaker tried his hardest to argue his way out the predicament he was in but Big Bill was having none of it.

'If your employee doesn't turn up to put the bets in the clock bag, don't f***ing blame me, the punter,'

'Well, don't you think it's a bit suspicious?' butted in Mr Arms Folded.

'Keep your f***ing trap shut, or I'll fill it up for you,' said Bill.

The bookmaker turned to my old man. 'You're to blame for this f**k-up, Larry.'

My dad went ballistic and went for the bookmaker, and the minder went for dad. I went for the minder and Bill ended up being the peacemaker. The bookmaker was adamant he wouldn't pay up.

Bill told him bluntly, 'If you don't pay me out my f***ing winnings in ten minutes I'll have fifty hairy-arsed iron fighters' (steel erectors) 'in here and I won't be responsible for any damage that they will undoubtedly create.'

The bookmaker, realising he was on another loser (the first one being my creativity) paid up. My dad and I had a right old laugh on the coach home, but now we had to find a new bookie. When I got home I told Lena the good news. She was over the moon.

'How much do you think you will get, Ed?' she asked.

I explained the situation, with Bill demanding half of the winnings, but I said, 'I would expect at least half of the remaining money. After all, if it wasn't for me, no one would have got anything.'

I didn't mention anything to my dad for a couple of weeks about the money, as he was making arrangements to deal with another bookie. We often met up at the monthly meetings of the Union of Construction Workers, which was held at the Winding Way Working Men's Club in Dagenham. As was the norm when we all got together, most of us got tanked up and tonight was no exception.

As my old man and I staggered our way home, I mentioned the winnings. 'When am I going to get my share, Dad?' I asked.

My dad answered me. 'Your share? What share?'

'My share of the winnings,' I said. 'If it hadn't of been for me, you wouldn't have got anything.'

'Well, you can kiss my arse,' he said and began to walk away

'You no good f***ing bastard,' I said.

He turned back towards me and lifted his fist as if to strike me, but without giving him the chance to hit me I retaliated with a terrific blow to his head, knocking him onto the bonnet of a parked car. The blow knocked him sparko.

I walked home crying my eyes out, not because of the sight of my poor old dad sprawled over the bonnet of a car but because of the way he treated his three sons. As far as he was concerned we were shit. That's why we were all rebellious.

My dad was a man's man, he would rather be in the company of men than his family. He never came to see me when I was evacuated to Wales and I remember he used to use the belt on us frequently. One particular instance I will always remember was when he was on his sticks (due to his 60-foot fall), when I had a fight with a boy in our street. At the time I had a very large carbuncle on the back of my neck. The boy's mother came to our house with the boy and complained to my dad about me fighting her son. My dad wasn't much of a communicator with women, he seemed to get embarrassed when approached by them.

'You little bastard,' he said to me and hit me several times with his walking stick, which caused the carbuncle to burst, causing blood and other crap to spew out of the wound like a miniature volcano.

The mother of the other boy then intervened. 'Mr Cogger, what are you doing?' She hadn't expected an assault like that to be the outcome of her complaint.

When I got home, Lena saw that I was upset and asked what the problem was, I explained what had happened.

'Don't worry love, it will look better in the morning, you'll see.' We had settled down in bed, when there was an almighty banging on the front door.

'It's him,' I said to Lena. 'The bastard's followed me. Don't make a sound.'

We hid in the kitchen, and our kids, his grandchildren, were beginning to cry. He was shouting out at the top of his voice, screaming, 'Come out you cowardly bastard, don't hide behind her.' He had quietened down a bit and I thought he had gone when I heard the letter box rattle. I thought he was after the key which was attached to a piece of string hanging from a nail on the front door, but luckily I had wrapped the string around the doorknob.

Suddenly, a 12-inch carving knife came through the letter box, and waving it about fanatically, he made it most clear what he would do if he got hold of me. Eventually he left, screaming profanities as he staggered away.

I never went back to work on the power station again. We wanted to move after the problem with my old man at the flat, and after about six months we were offered a lovely two up, two down corner house, which we immediately accepted.

We didn't (which was a relief for Lena) use the sweep's van to move this time; we hired a proper removal van. The location was ideal for us. The house was situated in a row of four houses and had a side gate in Rainham Road North. My mate Dougie Price (a welder at Tilbury Power Station where I had worked) lived opposite, and Sandie Shaw the pop star lived just up the road. Dougie nicked (with me) the two Stetsons belonging to 'you know who' some years earlier.

I had some good news from my solicitor relating to the claim I had made against my previous employers, who had admitted liability for the accident I had, resulting in an injury to my spine. They offered me £1,600, a fortune in those days. I was advised by the solicitors to reject the offer, which I did and they came back with a better offer, £1,950, which I gratefully accepted. We were rich! Well, that was rich in those days. The first most extravagant thing I did was to go out and buy a nearly new Ford Zephyr. I was lucky to have passed my driving test driving my dad about when he was in the money. It was a beautiful-looking car, a dark racing green colour, with a bench seat in the front for three, a column gear change box and a three-seat bench seat in the back. It was my pride and joy.

When we used to go out in it, Lena was Lady Penelope, who used to say to me, 'Onwards Parker.' I used to reply, 'Yes, me Lady.' Little Eddie was Virgil, Tracey was Scott and they all used to cry out 'Onwards, Thunderbirds' as we set out on a journey. Happy, happy days.

34

A New Beginning

Our lives had now become vastly improved, financially. Although I was now officially classed as disabled and was paid a disability benefit, I was allowed to work in a light work environment. I contemplated what I would be able to do.

I had so far in my life tried my hand at many things: at school I worked with the milkman, helping him before school, selling newspapers after school. I worked in the bookmaker's office with the beautiful aroma of Miss Thomas (wiggly bum), my teacher, whiffing around the office. Then there was my stint as a runner for my Dad, getting nicked on my first day. And my three years in the Merchant Navy on the *Royal Sovereign*, the Thames pleasure boat, with Lennie Wiltshire and Ginger Walford, when I nearly drowned. Then there was the stinking old tanker the *Esso Bristol*, another near-death experience; followed by my journeys to Australia. Next, my terror when I started on my first sheeting job and was shown what ducking meant. Then the moment of fear when I fell and slipped a disc, and the extreme embarrassment of being strung up naked to be plastered by a very bisexual plasterer of Paris (and I don't mean the city). Not to mention my time as a tea boy bookie's runner, who cunningly ripped off the bookie.

I knew what I wanted to be: a bookie. I had a flash car, a beautiful blonde wife, and potential. My dad was still working at the power station, and we had begun to speak again so I asked him if he would fancy collecting the bets for me. My brother was working on the same site and he was also taking bets, so I gave them a better offer than they were already getting, and they accepted.

I rented an office in East Ham and had a Racing Results System put in. I gradually built up the business, but as betting shops weren't about in those days, one could only take credit bets and these would be settled at the end of a week. On the other hand, bets that were taken on the sites were illegal, as were the street bookmakers, so that's why we used clock bags, with the money handed over with the bet and the bag was sealed before the first race.

I had quite a few runners working for me eventually, and became quite successful. After a couple of years betting shops were made legal and my business virtually collapsed. I still hung on for a while, but things were getting desperate and I had to sign on the dole. The lowest point came when a punter came up to me as I was signing on and said, 'What you doing here, Ed? I've just put a bet on with your brother.' I made some excuse that I had been called in about my disability benefit, and made a hasty retreat.

Unfortunately when my dad started as a street bookmaker he never had the foresight to expand his business. He loved to enjoy the trappings that went with his status in the locality, i.e. the Cherry Tree pub, the flash car, the Crombie overcoat, the Stetson hat, and Mum done up to the nines – she used to wear a real fox fur over her shoulders, and they really were a handsome couple. But as my dad swanned about, his rivals took advantage of the changes that were being made to the licensing laws that were being brought in, mainly betting shops.

Me, Lena, Bill Claridge (a local greengrocer who ended up a bookmaker and a good friend) and publican Freddie Cooper.

His main rival at that time was Mark Lane, who allegedly was supposed to have been treated more leniently than others in the area by the police (he even eventually bought the police station that had closed down and made it into his head office). Tommy Jennings had moved to Harlow and became Harlow Bookmakers. A local greengrocer, an old pal of mine, Bill Claridge, even applied for a licence and got one. By this time my dad was finished. Bill is still going 40 years on. Mark Lane eventually sold out to Corals. My poor old dad, who had started it all in about 1945 when Tommy Jennings (Patsy Martin) never came back from the cop shop, died penniless.

My final humiliation, and the end of my bookmaking career, came one day when there was a complete white-out (snow) of all racing in Britain. My brother Alec, who at the time was still collecting the bets at the power station, unfortunately took some bets from some hairy-arsed steel erectors who would have had a bet on anything. Alec, unaware that all racing had been abandoned, still took the bets as he normally would. He then brought the sealed bag home to me. I would normally take the bag to the office to settle any bets. However, as racing had been abandoned I did not expect to have to settle any bets, just return the stakes, as obviously no racing meant all bets were void.

However…! These thick erectors had sorted the most out-of-the-way, illegal dog racing flapping track there was to have a bet: Manchester White City. I knew then that I was in trouble, as it was a winning bet coming to more than £100, which I didn't have. When I told Alec that we didn't take bets from that track and the bets were void, he was stunned.

'F**k me Ed, what are we going to do? We'll be slaughtered. You will have to tell them that no one takes bets from illegal tracks. They're bound to ask for a rule book, and thanks to your stupidity you haven't even got one,' he said.

I said, 'I will go and get some printed. You try and fob them off until I get some done, just tell them that it is a flapping track, and is not a recognized track by the authorities.'

'I dunno, it's always me who has to do f***ing dirty work,' he moaned.

'Shouldn't have taken the bet,' I replied.

I got the rules printed, and even that was a f**k-up. The printer asked how many I wanted. I replied 'Just ten.'

'Ten? You're having a f***ing laugh, mate, ain't yer?' He stared at me in amazement. 'Do you know how long it takes me to set up the type? Especially in the tiddly little print you want, I can hardly see them.'

'What's the minimum you can do and how much are you going to charge me?' I asked.

He could see he wasn't going to earn a fortune out of me. 'Fifty for twenty-five quid,' he said.

F**k me I thought that will just about skint me. I had no option but to agree. 'When will they be ready?' I asked.

'F**k me, mate, anyone would think your life depended on them.'

Little did he know he could be right. I felt sorry for Alec, poor little sod, he would now be trying to explain to them why their bet was void. If it was me I would be well choked if I was expecting £100-plus winnings, only to be told the bet was void.

My office was on the second floor of a three-storey building. The office next door was occupied by three well-spoken young men who had a right scam going on. As I can remember, the scam was to look up in the phone book an office with a large typing pool, and ask the person on the other end of phone if they could speak to the person who ordered the carbon copy paper for the office; usually the person's name was given.

The young men next door then would send a bill with the name of the person who supposedly ordered the carbon copy paper to the Accounts Office. If they got two replies out of ten, with three of them working the phones, they were onto a good little earner. However I never did find out what the little scales in their office were used for. They didn't say goodbye either, when two heavies paid them a visit. Still, I had my own problems to worry about.

Alec phoned me up later in the day to say that the hairy-arsed erectors were on the way to the office – either to wish me all the best or to give me a good kicking. The latter, I thought. I couldn't leave the office then, as I might have met them in the street, so I sat tight.

It was quite dark when I heard raised voices in the road outside the office. Looking down, standing well away from the window, I saw four figures. 'Where the f**k's this office?' one was saying to the others. I had already been down the stairs to lock the front door. You couldn't tell one office from the other as there were so many of them. They hung around for about an hour and then left.

I gave Alec 'The Rules of Racing' to give to the hairy arses, said goodbye to my cosy little office, and then started to look around for my next venture.

35

A Change of Direction

Lena and I decided we had to make a change; the bookmaking career was now dead in the water and I could see I was now treading the same path as my old man. After discussing various possibilities, we came to the conclusion that as a lot of friends of ours had gone into the licensing trade, we should try and give it a go, especially as Lena didn't drink and had a terrific personality. We eventually applied to the Romford Brewing Company for a position as trainee managers.

Although Lena had a wonderful bubbly personality and could talk the hind leg off a donkey, she was concerned that her lack of education would let her down. She was, innocently, the dizziest of the dizzy blondes and she was genuinely loved by everyone who came into contact with her. Even the hierarchy of the brewery became enchanted with her when we had our job application interview, urging her not to change her personality, as it would be an asset for them.

My army career as a chef held us in good stead, as the breweries were now branching out into the catering field. The training programme entailed training for six weeks, learning in a pub, and also going to a school in Boreham Wood to learn the administration and law of the trade. We would then, if we were accepted, go on to become relief managers. We asked around the family to see if they could help to look after the boys whilst we trained, and our two boys stayed with their grandparents whilst we did our training.

The Church Elm Pub situated on the corner of the Heathway Shopping Centre, Dagenham was our designated training pub. This was ideal for me as most people knew me there. The pub was one of the toughest in the area. Many of my family used the pub, one being a well-known character, my cousin Henry Woolf (Woolfie) as he was known.

Henry was a great guy, a really lovely man. He, like the rest of us in the family, liked his drink, and he was in the Church Elm pub most days of the week. If not, he would be at one of the dog tracks in the area. He was often seen around Dagenham, walking his greyhounds. He was about 15 years older than me, and knew Lena's family very well as he was the son of my aunt Jess, my mum's sister who I mentioned earlier. He, like his brother Pearl, had been in the Navy but had come through the war unscathed, unlike his brother (who was only one of 25 to survive the sinking of the HMS *Wakeful*).

Unfortunately he came to a terrible, tragic death. He now lived on his own as his mum and dad had passed on. He had been out to walk his dogs (stopping to have a few rums at the Church Elm pub) but fell asleep in front of a gas fire and he and the dogs were found dead, having basically roasted to death.

There was one piece of shit who didn't know me too much, who got a bit flash on our first day at the pub. This one particular individual asked who I was, and I didn't give him my name as I wanted to see what his reaction would be when I eventually told him. He gave me an order to pull up, which I did, and told him the price it came to. Pointing at his nose he said, 'Take it out of that, prick.' I had been warned by the governor, Les Lees (the most respected licensee in the game) that I should expect this form of intimidation, and I was to deal with it – which I did. I went through the bar flap and asked him for the money he owed. He went to punch me and stopped short: he had recognized who I was. 'Try that again, prick, and I'll flatten you.' He was never a problem again.

There was a lot of intimidation in those days in the pubs, and you had to be a strong-willed person to survive as a publican. Obviously, for your wife it was doubly so, as she had the worry of how her kids were handling the separation, and to concentrate on all the training difficulties at the same time.

The Church Elm Pub was a very difficult pub to run, even for the hardest of publicans, such as Les Lees. I can remember on one occasion when a spate of demands were being made on the bar staff – the old con trick of ordering a large order, giving the barmaid £1 and insisting she was given £10 and demanding the change, with the poor barmaid told in no uncertain terms what would happen to her if she didn't comply. This resulted in Les having a string of bad stocks; if a publican had three bad stocks on the run he would be out of a job.

As Les was a senior and well-respected manager, the brewery decided to call in the police. A meeting was called by the brewery and police and a plan was drawn up where plain-clothes police would act as customers, and area managers as bar staff would work the bar. I, a trainee manager, was now on the other side of the fence. The Heathway Gang were not involved in this scam; as the old saying goes, don't shit on your own doorstep if you can shit on someone else's, and I have no doubt that this practice did happen in other pubs, as I was to find out later as a landlord of my own pubs over the next 20 years. On the night in question my wife and I were working the public bar, as the lounge cum music bar was where the scam was being perpetrated.

The first incident occurred when one of the persons involved in the fiddle said to a barman/copper, 'That was a tenner I gave you then, mate.'

'No, it was a pound note,' came the reply.

The scammer's mate then butted in. 'No, it was definitely a tenner he gave you.'

The tension began to mount, and suddenly a bottle was thrown, hitting my area manager, Ken Smith, on the head. He was knocked senseless and suffered severe head injuries. The plain-clothes police then entered the affray, calling on their uniformed colleagues who were positioned at the Doctor Who police box, with its blinking blue light on the top at the bottom of Heathway Hill. Yes, *Doctor Who* was about in those days (William Hartnell). There were quite a few injured on that particular night – that was about the norm for the Church Elm Pub – but the injury to the area manager was quite serious. He was in a coma for a while. His assailants were arrested and sentenced to a prison term. Unfortunately he died many years later, as I understand, of a blood clot or stroke.

On most nights the pub was like a saloon bar in an old cowboy film, a fight a night. No bouncers then, it was just you and the missus. We were lucky that we started our training in the Church Elm Pub, as everyone knew us. Lena, who had lived on the corner house about eight houses from the Church Elm Pub was well known firstly as the little ice cream girl, and then as the beautiful usherette who looked like Doris Day.

The six weeks we did at the Church Elm Pub soon passed, as we attended the Brewery Training School two days a week, which was a respite for the both of us. My participation in the running of a public house would entail the cellar work, maintaining the beers to the highest standard, understanding of bookkeeping and financial know-how, stocktaking, and some knowledge of the licensing laws, etcetera. Lena, who would be responsible for the catering side of the business, had to learn all the ins and outs from making a cheese roll to setting up a banquet for hundreds. Luckily the former was the more likely in the pubs we ran.

Now my Lena, who is loved by most people for her caring nature, including (as I have previously said) the top brass of the brewery, has one big fault: her ripe Cockney accent. I remember that on our Passing Out Day all the ladies had to do a presentation of what they had learnt on their courses. Eventually it came to Lena's turn (which I was dreading). Her presentation was 'How to make a ham sandwich'. I was rolling up with laughter at her inspirational choice. But what followed was even more hilarious: instead of a Dot Cotton-type impersonation coming out of her mouth, Lena, addressing one of the other trainee landladies, tried to posh it up a bit, in a Mrs Hyacinth Bouquet manner.

If you can imagine a typical Cockney voice coming out posh, this is what it sounded like: 'Josephine, this is how to make a ham sandwich. You take two slices of white bread, lay them down on a flat surface' – good idea – 'and spread some margarine over them,' – what, no butter? – 'you then lay two lettuce leaves, preferably from the heart,' – whose heart? – 'and then a slice of ham on top, put the other slice of bread on top and cut the sandwich diagonally and garnish to make it presentable.'

After about four months of training we did our first relief, taking a pub over, lock, stock and barrel as the saying goes, whilst the manager took his holidays. The pub was the Maypole at Colchester, right next to the Army barracks. The procedure is that on the morning of the start of the manager's holiday, a stock of all the sales is itemised. The manager, the relief manager and a stock taker take stock of all the saleable goods, beers, wines and spirits etcetera, and sign to declare everything is correct. I had been warned many times of the fiddle managers get up to and was very diligent on checking the stock, but I was still turned over.

The manager, before going on holiday, had hidden eight crates of empty light ales under other full crates, and as the stock taker hadn't noticed this, it meant I would be heading for a bad stock. So, on his return from holiday, I turned the tables on him by leaving the same empty cases on his stock result. He couldn't very well accuse me of leaving them amongst the stacks of crates as he had done to me; he must have accepted that he had been turned over by an inexperienced trainee, as I never heard anything from the brewery or him. But it did teach me a very important lesson: never to trust anyone again, only my immediate family.

After about four months of going around the circuit, learning the trade and gaining experience, we were to find out just how ruthless the breweries were. We were informed that we would be relieving a manager who had been dismissed from the Beacon Public House which was about 100 yards from our council flat. This would be ideal for us, as Lena would be able to go home every night, and she would be able to have the boys at home and take them to school, and then come to the pub to help me.

I knew the sacked manager very well. He told me he had been sacked, with his wife, immediately, for having a bad stock result. He had three young children and could not keep his eye on the staff, who in those days had the opportunity to take money from the tills if the manager had been distracted by a problem, which obviously he had with three young children. He was escorted from the pub by area managers, carrying a baby in his arms. That was to remain in my mind for the next 20 years. I didn't think a major brewing company could be as callous as that, but they were, and probably still are.

Over the course of the next 18 months, we did many reliefs at a variety of public houses, some almost unmanageable, others fight-a-night jobs, others what you might call normal.

36

The Thatched House, Barking

Eventually we were offered our own pub, the Thatched House, Barking. It was about a mile from the Church Elm, our training house. We went in with a bang, literally: it was 5th November 1969, Fireworks Night.

As previous experience had taught us, we refused to take the outgoing manager's stock, as the manager had put down a deposit and he would lose it if his stock was a bad one. In the past we had experience of a licensee filling empty whisky bottles with cold tea, vodka bottles with

At the start of Lena's battle against alchoholism.

water, and barrels of beer with water, so we had to take care when taking over from a sacked manager.

Well, opening time came; we opened at 11 o'clock, expectantly waiting for the first customer to walk through the doors. In they came, four of them.

'You the new guvnor?' they asked.

'Yes, I am,' I replied. 'Why?'

'Well, we usually get a free drink from the guvnor,' one replied.

'Not from me,' I said, and with that he threw a bottle through one of the windows and they ran off, with me and Lena in hot pursuit.

We didn't catch them, or allow them back in again. But I had upset the brother of one of them, who had allegedly killed another hardcase by hanging him up by the neck on the spikes of park railings. He was serving time at the moment for another offence; he was an alleged psychopath, a really dangerous man. So that was a fine start to our managerial careers.

More fun was to follow when we were due to open for the evening session.

'Come on you bastards, open up.' It was Frank Cross, who eventually became a very good friend to Lena and I. 'F**k me, mate, I could have been on my second pint by now.' Giving me a furtive grin as he said it.

He was Terry Venables's uncle; all his aunts and uncles, who lived locally, used our pub as did his cousins. A smashing family.

I first realised, when we were being interviewed for the Thatched House by the area manager Ken Smith, that we were being given a very low staff wage allowance: there was no money for cleaners or a cellar man. On querying this he replied, 'Build the trade up and you will get the extra wages you want.' That was it, I had no choice but to get the two boys to clean and polish the tables in the bars before they went to school. Lena had to mop and bucket the bars and toilets. I had to do the cellar and the bottling up, and I would long remember the way we were treated then – slave labour.

Well, we got on with it and we started music nights, which proved a great success and the takings increased, so we were able to take on more staff.

Obviously, with the increase in customers, the pub used to attract a lot more unwelcome characters. Most of the Heathway Gang used to come in, especially Lennie Wiltshire, who I deeply thank for the help and support he gave Lena and I over the coming years. We had many good years, and many difficult times. Our boys Tracey and Eddie were 11 and 14 when we had our first serious problem.

On this particular occasion a customer had a reason to complain about being short-changed. I questioned the barmaid involved and she said he had only given her £1. I then realised that the con tricksters were working my pub. I remonstrated with him and told him to 'Piss off'. His reaction was to strike me a blow in the eye. I ran to another exit to confront him.

He must have thought I was running away, because he turned around to his mate, laughingly saying, 'He's had it away, no good bastard', not realising I was coming up behind him, I tapped him on the shoulder, and as he turned around I nutted him straight on his hooter with the best centre-forward's header I have ever delivered, splattering his conk all over his face.

Lena and the two boys came around the bar and jumped on the bloke while I went to see if his mate wanted any of the same, which he evidently didn't. In the meantime a barman had phoned the police, who arrived surprisingly quickly, as they weren't usually too quick to arrive at pub brawls: free pints, yes; bribing poor hard-working publicans, yes; but pub fights, no.

The trouble-maker was arrested for an assault on me, and attempting to obtain money by deceit. He also made a complaint against me of assaulting him. I realised that his injuries were much worse than mine, so Lena came up with the idea of making my eye injury look worse by using make-up, which she was a dab hand at, and taking a photograph of it. It turned out brilliantly.

As the case wasn't to be heard for a while, my injury would heal up, but I would have the photographic evidence as proof of my injuries. He eventually pleaded guilty and had a hefty fine imposed. I received damages and was commended by the court for my actions. Lena had a big kiss from me for her make-up skills.

In fact I hadn't been aware of any police bribery (apart from the days of street bookmaking, when they used to come to my old man's house for their bung, for informing him when they would come to nick a runner). I did, however, have a very vicious pair of detectives pay me a visit soon after I had taken the pub over. They introduced themselves and said they were investigating a case of publicans receiving stolen tea. I knew this was a ruse to get a free drink on the house, as they would put it. But I knew this would be the thin edge of the wedge, so I said, 'You won't find any tea here, mate, but you're welcome to look around if you want.' They looked surprised at this offer, but they couldn't refuse it, as they realised that a double bluff had been worked on them.

I invited them into the kitchen and asked where they would like to look. They shrugged their shoulders, so I opened the pantry door and said, 'Well this is where we keep the food, you're welcome to look.'

They walked in and I heard a typical Jack Warner (*Dixon of Dock Green*) 'Hello, hello, what have we got here then?'

Looking in I saw they had an OXO tin in their hands, and guess what was in it? Tea, about 2 lbs worth.

'Where's this lot come from then?' one asked.

I was astounded. 'F****ng Peark's Grocers, that's where, you stupid bastard.'

'No need for that kind of language, sir. We would like to search your living quarters now.'

'What for?' I asked. 'That tin is what the staff use to make their tea.'

It was futile arguing with them. Finding no tea in the living quarters, they asked to look into the cellar and spirit locker.

'Have you got the key to the spirit locker please guv?' they asked.

'Why? I asked.'

'Well you could have tea hidden away in there,' they said.

'I could have it hidden it up my arse as well,' I replied.

'Might have to look up there too,' one said.

I finally found out there was no tea nicked: it was just a ruse to get into the spirit locker. They informed me I was lucky not to be nicked for abusive language against two officers going about their legal duty, and proceeded to take two bottles of whisky as presents from mine host. No wonder there were hundreds of whisky bottles filled up with cold tea on the back rows of many a spirit locker. Probably the same tea they were looking for.

In those days pubs used to have little private bars, which most of the elderly used. Lena loved older people, and as they knew us as locals, they loved the banter she had with them. While we were at the Beacon doing the emergency relief, there was one particular character who was a regular in the bar, Irish Mary, who lived in our flats, and Lena and her got on like a house on fire.

One day she remarked that Lena was looking a bit off-colour, and she should have a nice glass of Guinness, to which Lena replied that she didn't drink alcohol. 'Well, you should have a tonic of some kind, try a Wincarnis,' said Mary. 'That should put some colour back in your cheeks.' Well, Lena took her advice and bought a bottle to have a glass

Lena on sick leave during her first bout of depression.

now and again when she felt a bit down in the dumps. That bottle of seemingly innocent drink was to lead her into the deepest depths of despair, nervous breakdowns, suicidal thoughts and mental homes. Worst of all I, due to concentrating on making a success of our career, was ignorant to the fact that my darling little Lena was sinking into an abyss of fear and eventually alcoholism which was to last many years.

The first I ever knew of this matter was when we had a two-week break and she went to the doctor and explained her situation to him. After examining her he immediately arranged for her to go to hospital, as she was suffering from alcohol poisoning. She had covered it up so skilfully that I never had an inkling that she even drank alcohol. It was heart-breaking as the two boys and I saw a beautiful wife and mother make her way alone to the bus stop, a little bag of clothes in her hands, on the way to Warley Mental Hospital to fight the demons that were trying to destroy her. I didn't even have a car to take her to hospital.

I was desperately trying to keep her illness to just the boys and myself, as the brewery were very callous, as was shown by their treatment of the manager at the Beacon, when he and his family were dismissed instantly. Who knows, perhaps his wife was suffering from depression, having had three children so quickly. I managed to keep Lena's illness

155

just in the family. If the brewery had found out that there was a problem, we also would have been shown the door.

I was lucky that the area manager was on holiday at the time, so I could visit Lena. I was gutted when I saw my little Lena, she was barely conscious. She had intravenous tubes up her nose and in her veins, and she looked so ill that I feared for her life. She had a tube going into a bag that contained a green substance that was coming from her body. The doctor confirmed that she was suffering from alcoholic poisoning and was lucky to be alive. She was also having a nervous breakdown, which I had also been unaware of.

Although they were young – Tracey was approximately 11 years old and Eddie about 14 – the boys understood the problem that their mother was suffering from. They knew how sick she was by the tubes and other things that were protruding from her body which they saw when visiting her.

Lena recovering at home.

Although Lena appeared outwardly to be full of fun and a laugh-a-minute type, she was basically a very insecure person. I came along with my brashness and Jack the Lad attitude, and the excitement of being one of the Heathway Boys' girlfriends meant she enjoyed that and it fetched her out of her shell, but she was still that little girl who dreamt of being Doris Day singing 'Once I had a Secret Love', whilst all the lads tried to nick her ice creams.

Once she had got somewhat better, I said I thought that it was probably the wrong job for us, and we discussed what I could do if we didn't carry on. I explained that I wouldn't be able to go back into steel erecting because of my disability; bookmaking was now legal and betting shops were opening up all over the place, anyway all the young mathematicians had been snatched up by bookmakers – people like me who worked out bets from a little fixed odds book were long gone. Lena said she would give it another go.

37

Back to the Thatched House

While Lena was in the hospital, I took on a bar cellarman, Tommy Tucker. He was well into his seventies but as sprightly as an old 50-year-old. He had lodged around Barking for many years and was well pleased to have the rooms and food that came with his job. It would also give me time to spend with Lena and the boys. From a young age the boys had worked in our pubs without any moaning. They helped Lena and me with the bottling up, cleaning the bars, polishing the tables, cellar work, etcetera, before they went to school.

Lena singing 'Once I had a Secret Love' – aged about 26.

Mr Michael Carraban presents us with a prize for Best Pub. He was very understanding of Lena's problems.

Lena was coping as best she could under the circumstances; she was now on a cocktail of drugs prescribed by her doctor, as she was suffering from severe depression. To make things worse her father, who she idolised, was dying from emphysema. She was with him when he died and was heartbroken.

The company, which now knew of her depression, was very sympathetic to her, mainly due to a new managing director, Michael Carraban, who portrayed a more human side to the brewing industry. He realised that wives were mothers and that motherhood meant more to them than being landladies, especially when they had young children; more so when they weren't even on the wage bill.

The death of Lena's father was a shattering blow to her, and she became even more depressed, if that was possible. Unfortunately, even with my sons' and my own diligence, Lena took to the bottle again and was admitted back to Warley Hospital. Fortunately Tommy Tucker was now there to look after the pub while I visited her. She was there for about three weeks, after which I took her home again.

Eventually Lena recovered, but was warned that if she drank again it could kill her. She vowed that she would never drink again and with

Us with customers in fancy dress in the Thatched House.

thanks to God, she hasn't touched a drop for the past 35 years. She still takes lots of medication for her depression, but the demon drink has gone forever.

We had now turned the Thatched House into a theme house. It had had a complete renovation, it had music every night and was now known as the Reflections Bar, due to the mirrors that were placed in the bar and positioned to reflect off each other. The pub had now become the busiest pub in town.

It was alleged that some managers who ran similar types of establishments used to use devious methods to increase their own income, which at that time was very low. Also, a manager's job was very insecure, as every month a stock take was carried out. If it was a bad stock you were giving a warning; a second bad stock and you would be given a final warning. What some of these managers resorted to was to keep all the empty spirit bottles, add them all up, and take one in three for themselves and go to the local off licence and buy (say if the manager had sold 60 bottles of spirits) 20 at off sales price, which would be half the optic price, enabling him to put the bottles back into stock and put the other half in his pocket. This was also done by buying in kilns of beer; to get the cost of buying these items, the manager would have stayed up

161

half the night ringing the tills around, to get to where he wanted to get his money out.

Well, in those days there wouldn't be any managers, they would have all been sacked, what with the police wanting their bung, stock-takers taking the odd bottle or two home to please the wife to be on a promise, the local villains working the old protection racket, luckily not with me. We were lucky that we were well known in the area, as there was quite a lot of villainy going on in the locality, including murder.

Behind the Thatched House was a fenced-off area that probably would have been a large garden, that the company had rented to a group of about six fairground families. The headman was a massive man who was called Swaley Remblance. His three sons were nearly as big, and he and his family thought a lot of Lena and I and the two boys. He remarked many a time that I was to call on him if I had a need to, for which I was very grateful. He also invited Lena and I to the Annual Showman's Dance at the Lyceum in London.

There I witnessed the biggest brawl I have ever seen in my life. It was just like the fights in the old cowboy films: men were jumping and throwing themselves off the balconies onto the heaving mass below. Some were unluckily enough to jump just as the fighters below spread apart from each other. I bet Joe Loss and his band were shitting bricks and feeling somewhat peeved that no one was dancing.

I said to Swaley, 'Good night?'

He replied, 'It's always the same.'

As the business and notoriety of the pub was becoming more popular, it began to attract a more unsavoury clientele and I needed to take on more staff, especially men. One man I interviewed was a local character called Tommy Honeyman who worked during the day as a morgue attendant at the local hospital. His brother was in the SAS in Malaya. Apparently he mistakenly shot and killed a young boy. As a result of this he lost all of his hair and gained the nickname of 'Nut Nut'. I didn't know if he was called this because his mates said he was a nutcase or because of his bald head. I was soon to find out.

I did employ Tommy and he was a very good barman, but he did like his beer and eventually I had to let him go. One night, it was New Year's Eve, the pub was heaving, everyone was clamouring for a drink. Tommy was at the front of the bar causing trouble because he couldn't get served, and started yelling obscenities at me. 'F***ing no good bastard, call yourself a landlord?' With that I couldn't contain myself and gave him such a whack across the bar that I knocked him out, but as the pub was so full he couldn't fall down. As the music was in full swing he was the first person I have seen involuntary doing the 'Hokey Cokey' upright around the bar, his head resting on someone's shoulder.

The locals informed me that 'Nut Nut' Alan Honeyman, who had been discharged from the Army on medical grounds, wouldn't think a lot of me sticking it on his brother. I just replied, 'What will be, will be, there was nothing I could do about it now.'

Eventually he turned up, he looked worse than I had been expecting. His nose was splattered all over his face, his shiny bald head was a jigsaw puzzle of scars. His demeanour was pretty scary. Apparently he had a party piece in which he would chew on a broken glass, which he proceeded to do. He looked me in the eyes, bloodied mouth agape.

'Did you stick it on my f***ing brother?' he asked. His friends, who were crowded around him like a pack of grinning hyenas, stepped back a few paces.

I looked him straight back in the eyes, my hand reaching out for the sawn-off snooker cue I kept under the counter. 'I'm afraid I did,' I replied.

He looked somewhat perplexed, looked at me, gave an almighty roar, and proceeded to rip the fire extinguisher off the wall and started to chew on the rubber hose, without success. I asked him if he was happy now.

'Well done, guv, he probably deserved it, no-good bastard.'

He asked if he could buy me a pint, which I accepted, and I bought him one back. From that day we were the best of friends. The hyenas couldn't believe it.

Apart from me having my physical altercations, on occasions Lena also had hers to attend to. We had had many requests by the customers who asked if we could get a jellied eel stall put outside the pub, which we thought was a great idea, so I bought a jellied eel stall which was a great success. Our youngest son Tracey ran it and shared the profits with his mum. One Sunday lunchtime I heard a commotion going on outside the pub and saw Lena go rushing out to the stall and start hitting a man who had apparently dragged our son by the arm across the Perspex counter, causing severe grazing.

Lena was a compulsive collector of gold and probably had enough gold rings for every day of the year; she wore one on every finger of her two hands and she looked like she was wearing knuckledusters. As she looked like she was getting the best of things I left her to it. Unfortunately the bloke's face was covered in blood caused by her rings and he had the misfortune of his gold watch coming off. He also had the indignity of watching as Lena stamped on it over and over again until it was ground to pieces. I could see that the pent-up feelings she had suffered over the years in Warley Hospital had now eased somewhat. Unfortunately that was no comfort to the bloke, who slunk away with his tail between his legs, as the saying goes.

The stall was such a success that Lena thought that as it was only used at weekends she could put it to some use during the weekdays. So she went to a warehouse and had a look around to see what would be a good seller on the stall. She came home with about a dozen highly coloured quilts and some women's clothes. She got the two boys and I to position the stall outside the pub on the pavement, which was adjacent to one of the busiest roads in the country, the A13. There was just one problem: every time a big lorry sped by, it nearly shook the stall to pieces, and the back-draught was so strong that we had to tie the stall to the pub railings. The stall did so well that Lena had to go to the warehouse two or three times a week.

In the meantime we were still having the odd bit of trouble. On one occasion one of my brother's in-laws started trouble. Lena went round the bar to stop it and I saw one of them kick her. I rushed out to go to her aid, as did some customers. I hooked one of them, who went down, and began to force the group out of the door. One of them was resisting strongly and he swung a punch at me, knocking me a bit dizzy, so I got hold of his head and pushed it hard against the door.

Unfortunately I didn't realise his head was pressing on the window of the door. Suddenly the window broke, forcing his head through the broken window, causing him to bleed profusely. The group then began to concentrate on him rather than on me, and rushed him to the hospital. My brother's brother-in-law then came back into the bar and said to me, 'I'll be back later and I'll shoot you.' I knew he was a nasty piece of work, so I would have to keep vigilant that night, which I did.

It was about two o'clock in the morning; I was sitting in the saloon bar, in the dark, when I saw a car pull into the forecourt. I had already warned Lena to be near the phone, ready to call the police in case he did anything drastic. He went to the boot of his car and took something out wrapped in a blanket; it was about 3 feet long and was shaped like a shotgun. I called to Lena to ring the police and turned back to see what he was doing. He was unwrapping the blanket; he then pulled back his arm and threw the object through the window. F**k me, I thought to myself, he's thrown a pipe bomb or something through the window. He then jumped into his car and had it away.

The police eventually arrived, asking what had happened. I explained that we had heard a smashing sound and came down and found the window had been broken. They asked if I had found what had been thrown through the window. I replied that I hadn't looked yet, and that I was waiting for them to arrive. Well, I didn't want to tell them I thought it was a shotgun.

They searched around and found it. It wasn't a gun, it wasn't a pipe bomb, it was a 3-foot-long wrench. They asked if I had had any trouble that night.

'Not out of the ordinary,' I replied.

'Well someone's broken your front door window,' one said as they left.

F**k it, I had forgotten that window.

The boys were growing up now: Eddie was just starting out as a trainee chef at Plaistow Hospital and Tracey was now about 14 years of age. He was a right little sod, but he had his head screwed on. He was earning a small fortune working on his jellied eel stall and helping his mum selling her quilts and clothes.

As I have mentioned before some managers were having difficulty in returning good stock results, and a system of manipulating figures was devised with the help of a few stock takers; it was called 'pass the parcel'. The system worked like this. The stock taker's office would ring up and inform you that you would be having a stock take on a certain day, so you would get everything prepared for him. But this gave the manager the opportunity to have a private stock taker in to do a stock for you. If you were down on your stock you could then go to a manager who had recently had a stock, and borrow from him what you wanted, returning it when you were due for your next stock take, or when you were able to go to your private retailer and buy some stock in. Hence the term 'pass the parcel'.

The 'pass the parcel' scam was finally exposed and the company set up their own enquiry. They drew in from the other areas of the company all the stock takers they had and without giving any warning to the managers, gave us an early morning call. The managers who did have a bad stock result were dismissed instantly; luckily I wasn't one of those.

About a mile from the Thatched House there was a private club, the Scruttons Farm Club. We sort of shared clientele, like all pubs and clubs in the area. The club was owned (or managed) by two brothers, the Maxwells, and their good friend Ronnie Reader. They were regular customers at my pub and used to put themselves about a bit, but they were always all right with me. Roy Shaw mentions the two brothers in his book, when he warned them off for a problem the owner was having with them. He says he later learned that he thought they were accused of a murder, but I had never heard this.

One of the pubs I used to visit a lot was the Brewery Tap in Barking: all of the company local managers used to meet up there on banking days, to catch up on all the local gossip. The manager there was a giant of a man – he was one of the policemen who was drafted in when the Church Elm was having the scam worked on it, as I mentioned earlier, and on his retirement he was offered a manager's position by the brewery. His name was Ron Cook.

What was most unusual about the pub was that his potman cum bouncer was a woman – who was nearly as big as Ron. I forget her first name, but her surname was Elmore and she was quite a character about town. However, she had a terrible tragedy that happened involving her son Davy Elmore. He, like his mum, was a big lump and allegedly used to put the frighteners on local people and businesses. Apparently one night he was sitting having a meal in a Turkish restaurant when a row erupted. He was enticed into a toilet, wherein someone charged in with a spear which had been taken off the restaurant wall, and thrust it into his chest, killing him. It was alleged that people who used my pub were involved in his killing but nothing was proved.

I had been in the Thatched House about ten years when I had to go to the doctor as I had been having a problem with my waterworks. He fondled my sausage and meat balls before proclaiming proudly that I didn't have a rupture. He then proceeded to put a rubber glove on his hand and he greased one finger. I had never had any medical intrusion (apart from parting my arse for the DDT to be squirted up my ring piece in the Army). I was somewhat perturbed as to what his intentions were. I was soon to find out.

'Bend over please, Mr Cogger,' he said. 'This might be somewhat uncomfortable.'

This what? I said to myself. Well, he got on with it and it did hurt. I thought I would rather be straight than gay and to suffer that pain regularly.

After the examination was over he said I had an enlarged prostate gland, which I had never heard of before. He explained that it could be treated with medication, but he would make an appointment for me to go to hospital for a more thorough examination.

The day arrived for me to go to the hospital, and as my name was called out trepidation set in. I hadn't felt any anxiety until that moment, then it struck me, I was going to be examined for cancer of the prostate. Now I was scared. As I entered the room, I glanced around and my heart must have missed a few beats, for what I saw frightened the life out of me. On the window sill were these long thin steel instruments with what looked like eye pieces on the end. My imagination running riot, I assumed that these were going to be pushed up the eye of my 'cock-a-doodle-loo'.

The doctor, seeing me eyeing these instruments up with fear in my eyes, said, 'Don't worry about those; we don't use those any more.'

Thank f**k for that, I said to myself; they looked more suitable for horses than men. I had to endure the middle finger job again. He must have had a thicker and longer finger than my own doctor, as the pain was twice as bad. I just hoped I wasn't going to get to enjoy it.

Anyway, the result was the same, an enlarged prostate gland, so it was hoped that medication could control it until it got so large that I would need an operation to remove it. About 30 years later when I eventually stopped pissing I had to have it operated on.

We had been at the Thatched House pub for about eleven years now, and that was a record for any pub. In 1977 we decided to look for a home to buy for when we retired. Our search ended when we found a lovely bungalow in a little Essex village called North Fambridge, on the River Crouch. We agreed to buy the bungalow, and began to furnish it.

Unfortunately Lena was not feeling too well at the time we had agreed to buy the bungalow. She was having a lot of pain, as Les Dawson would have put it in his drag act character, gesturing down below, and miming. I don't know how to mime in print, but you get what I mean.

Our house in North Fambridge as it looked in 1977 and how it looked in 2009.

She went to the doctor and was sent to the hospital and was found to have a massive fibroid. She was told she would have to have an operation. She cried all the way home, as she didn't even know what a fibroid was. As a matter of fact, neither did I. She probably heard the words 'benign tumour', and that frightened the life out of her.

She had the operation, spent the day recovering, and when I went to see her the next day she was an apparition of beauty. Her blonde hair was combed around her face in a feathered style, stuck to the sides of her cheeks with soap. She wore a black negligee and black outer gown. The nurses said she had been preparing herself since early morning, I could well believe that. After Lena had left the hospital, she went to the bungalow to recuperate from her operation.

The company, aware that I wouldn't be able to run the pub on my own, sent a trainee couple to help me whilst Lena was recovering. This gave me the opportunity to spend a few days with her.

Two friends who used to visit us at the Thatched House were Josher Jones and his wife Joan; we had known them for many years. He had four sons, and he and the sons were all a bit tasty (they could handle themselves). Josh was a builder whose sons worked for him. A lot of his time was spent on his boat, and I used to go out fishing with him. What with the escapades I had in the merchant navy on the

Me and Roger Attewell on the Sea Lena.

oil tanker, I should have known better. Also good friends were Roger Attewell, a good muscled 17-stoner, and his brother Patsy, who was even bigger.

38

The Sea Lena

One day, as we were chatting in the pub, Josh asked me whether, seeing as we were living on the banks of the River Crouch, I would be interested in buying a boat, as he knew of one that was for sale where his boat was moored in Barking Creek. I said that I hadn't given any thought to buying a boat, but it seemed a good idea, as most people in the village owned a boat. I said I would come down to the creek to have a look at it. Now I knew that Josh was an optimist but this was taking it a bit too far, for tied up against the sea wall was what I could only describe as a wreck.

'You're having a laugh, Josh,' I said to him.

'Why? What's wrong with it? All it needs is a good clean-up, a couple of coats of paint, and it's got a brilliant Lindsey Perkins diesel engine. I can do that for you, no problem,' he said, nonchalantly.

'How much does he want for it?' I asked.

'Seven hundred and fifty,' he replied.

'Tell him I will give him six hundred and fifty, and no more,' I said. Josh was a lovable rogue, so he had, I assumed, put £50 on top for himself.

Well, I was now the proud owner of a wreck, but knowing Josh as I did, he would do a good job on it. After he had started working on the boat, Josh unfortunately had a heart attack, so it delayed the work for a couple of months.

Things were going well for us at the Thatched House, especially when one day an army lorry pulled onto the forecourt. A Sergeant jumped out and my heart sank as I thought that they had come for me for not reporting to the Territorial Army 20-odd years earlier.

'You the guvner?' he asked.

'Why?' I apprehensively responded.

'Well I'm looking for bed and breakfast for twenty Ukrainians for about six months. We are going to clear the Rainham Marshes of ammunition left over from the war.'

The Marshes was an area well known for artillery training. I asked, 'When they would be coming?'

'In about a month,' he replied.

I told him I would need a deposit, and we agreed a price. He said they wouldn't need anything special, remarking, 'They're only Ukrainian ex-prisoners of war who stayed behind to help us clear up the ammunition dumps.'

It was certainly a good result for us: 20 B&Bs for six months, we would earn a fortune, especially if the company didn't get to know about it. In those days, apart from the managers' living areas, the rest of the rooms had been left to rot. In those days everything was based on profit-making on beers and spirits, and no one seemed to have the common sense to think there was a lot of money to be earned in catering, letting rooms, etcetera.

In the Thatched House there were 12 rooms – six in the manager's quarters and six in another section of the pub – but they were in a dilapidated state of repair. So I got my dad in to decorate the rooms, and fitted them out with cheap second-hand furniture. They would sleep 16, and I also bought a cheap caravan to sleep four, and bingo, let the money roll in.

As far as the Ukrainians were concerned, they were in the lap of luxury, especially with Tommy Tucker serving them with his snuff-stained fingers (he was addicted to snuff). During the following six months, financially things couldn't have been better for us. We were raking it in from the Ukrainians, also from other means, such as the jellied eel stall, the quilts and clothes.

I was a bookmaker once, and one of my ambitions was to be a racehorse owner. One day I saw in the *Sporting Life*, the racing paper, an advert for shares in a race horse syndicate. I made enquiries, and Lena and I became the proud owners of a one part share in two racehorses, Pasadena and Mystic Princess. We went to see them every time they ran, but they were useless. However, as owners we were allowed to go into the Owners' Ring and rubbed shoulders with many dignitaries including the Queen Mother, down to the not-so-dignified stupid prat of a drunk, Oliver Reed, who after the racing was over, challenged his load of crap hangers-on to a final furlong race. This ended with him falling face first into a load of horse shit, which an obliging gee gee had deposited onto the grass as it (in its case) passed the losing post!

We also bought three greyhounds which we named Local Solo, Katie's Babylon and Gary's Enterprise. We had mixed luck with them, but it

Lena with one of our horses.

Katie's Babylon and Gary's Enterprise.

was fun. Our first, which we sent to the Romford Dog Track for trials, was Local Solo. A very speedy dog, but he had a tendency to break a good few lengths in front out of the traps and then wait for the others to catch up with him to have a fight (even our dogs had the family trait). The dog was banned for fighting, so we couldn't race him on any legal track.

Earlier I wrote of a famous wrestler of the late 1940s and early 1950s named Man Mountain Dean. After he had finished wrestling he opened a flapping track (illegal) on farmland he had somewhere near Tilbury, Essex that owners used to race dogs that had been barred from the legal tracks. The track consisted of a straight run of about 200 yards. He had an old wreck of a car engine which had been adapted to wind a long rope onto a drum of some kind when the engine was started up. A rugby ball was attached to the end of the rope, and at a great speed the rope and the ball, with two greyhounds chasing it, was wound around the drum to the finishing line.

We entered our dog and he won it tail first and fighting the other dog behind him. The enormous Man Mountain Dean, who was judge, steward and bouncer, and who was sitting on a stool which seemed to have disappeared up his arse, raised a very large megaphone to his mouth, shouting that our dog was disqualified and would never be allowed back again. I said to myself, f**k me, if it can't run at a shit hole like this we've no chance.

Our second dog, Gary's Enterprise, was somewhat better although very timid; he did manage to make the grade at Romford and was entered for his first race. Although he ran very well for an inexperienced dog, he came in last. In his second race he also came last. As we had lost quite a lot of money we asked the trainer, what the dog's chances were likely to be in its third race. He said, 'Well, you've seen what it's like; it's so timid it's frightened of its own shadow.' On the night, having heard the trainer's advice, it was the outsider at 33/1, so we left it alone. It f***ing pissed it. We phoned the trainer the next morning to ask him what the f**k was going on.

He said, 'I've got some other bad news for you, the kennel maid found him dead in his kennel this morning, he had died of a heart attack.'

I did my nut then. 'What a load of f***ing bollocks. You've got to be f***ing joking! Who's ever heard of a sodding dog dying of a heart attack? People die of heart attacks, not f***ing dogs.'

Finally we did have a change of luck with Katie's Babylon; she won

Proud owners of winner Katie's Babylon.

a few races, but our greatest thrill was when she won a trophy race at Ipswich Racetrack.

Lena, as the owner, eccentrically dressed in a gold lamé dress with her gold rings on every finger, gold sovereign chains around her neck, blonde hair, looking like a bullion robber's moll, went to collect the trophy, and in her best Queen's mimicry ('We are here today . . .' etcetera etcetera) she accepted the plastic trophy from a tubby little bookmaker who had donated the prize. Probably it cost a fiver.

While Josh was working on the boat, Lena and I went on our summer holidays. We always went to Mousehole in Cornwall where we had made friends many years earlier, with a family who owned a hotel called The Coastguard which overlooked the pretty little harbour.

Anyone who has been to Mousehole would probably have heard of the terrible tragedy that occurred one night when the coastguard were called out in horrific weather conditions to go to the assistance of a stricken ship. Unfortunately, they tried many times to get to the ship

175

Tracey and Eddie.

and finally they got too close to the vessel, which rose up high on a colossal wave and crashed down onto the helpless lifeboat, all lives being lost. Most of them belonged to the coastguard's pub choir, with whom we spent many a happy night singing along to old sea shanties.

We had left the two boys back at the pub. Eddie was now 17 and Tracey, like all teenagers, thought that going on holiday with parents wasn't the in thing. However, when we got back to the pub there was trouble brewing (and I don't mean as in beer).

Earlier I wrote of the psychopath who had allegedly killed a person by hanging him by the throat on a spiked railing. Apparently he had a relationship with one of the barmaids and, according to Tracey, was now demanding free drinks and money from her. Tracey, who always looked after our interests, knowing the ruthlessness of the brewery, told me what was going on. I spoke to the barmaid who admitted it and said she was frightened of this person, who intimidated her into doing it. Obviously I had to sack her on the spot.

In the evening I contacted Lennie Wiltshire and a few others and explained the situation. They knew him very well and said they would pay a visit that evening. When they came in, they discreetly positioned themselves where they wouldn't be seen. Tracey was with me behind the bar as the psychopath walked in. He ordered a bottle of light ale, poured it into a glass, put the bottle onto a table and called Tracey to go over to him.

'Did you tell your f***ing old man that I was getting free drinks and cash from my bird you, bubbling little bastard?' He picked the bottle up as he was ranting on.

Pushing Tracey away from him, I went to the other side of the bar to confront him; his wildly manic bloodshot eyes stared at me as I told him he was barred. With that, he swung the bottle at me. I managed to grapple with him, and as I did, someone struck him an almighty blow, knocking him to the ground and then followed a very, very severe kicking.

As he lay on the ground, bleeding profusely, his assailant leant over him and said, 'Danny, if you ever come in here again and mess with my friends, you'll never walk again.' Some years later we learnt he was dead. How he had died, and the cause, I never found out.

It was never the same again, however, and Lena suggested we make a move. The director, Mr Carraban, understood our position, especially as he had understood Lena's periods of depression. He also took into consideration we had served 13 years at the Thatched House, and no one could have served in a rougher house than that was, and for as long as we did, without at least getting a bloodied nose. We had a break due to us, so we went to the bungalow.

39

Back to the Boat

In the meantime Josh had finished the boat and we prepared to take it out of Barking Creek and sail down to the River Crouch. On board were Josh, Roger Attewell, myself, and Eddie and Tracey. I did remark to Josh that I was a bit concerned that we didn't have any navigation lights. He casually said, as he rolled a cigarette, that I wouldn't need any, as I wouldn't be going out in the dark. I thought to myself, I suppose he's right.

Well, we travelled up the Thames uneventfully, dropped Roger off on the way and made our way on to Southend. When we got there Josh said we would have to anchor up as the tide was against us now, so we could do a bit of fishing. We stayed there fishing for a couple of hours until the tide had turned, and then we set off on the second most terrifying experience I have ever had (the first being the collision on the tanker).

Apparently we set off when the ebb tide had begun to turn. What that means I'm f***ed if I know, but I do know that the boat began to toss and turn, one minute sitting high on top of a wave, and the next minute plunging to the depths of another. Water was pouring over the gunwales (sides) of the boat. The two boys were shitting themselves, as was I. Josh seemed somewhat worried.

As we had one of those little gas-filled hooters on board, I asked should I blow it. Josh looked at me incredulously. 'What the f**k do you think that's going to do? It's like a bleeding toy, you should dump it.' I felt quite put out at that, I had paid £3 for it.

We managed to manoeuvre to calmer waters as the sun was beginning to go down, and Josh positioned me on the bow of the boat and told me to look out for three buoys that would be marked Maplin 1, Maplin 2 and Maplin 3. As we were progressing towards our destination, the sun was rapidly sinking lower in the sky, and as we had passed Maplin 1, I was now having difficulty seeing the next buoy as the sun had sunk

Top Left: Lena on *Sea Lena.*

Top Right : Me on the stern.

Above: Roger, Tracey
and Eddie.

Right: Josh.

below the horizon on the onset of dusk. 'Can you see it yet?' asked Joss, I was just about to say no, when it appeared before us.

It was now very dark, and it didn't help not having any navigation lights, or even a torch. Still, that was Josh, he was so laid back that nothing seemed to worry him. He said that looking for the third buoy would be useless, so we would have to cut across the mouth of the Crouch between the buoys.

I f***ing knew that they don't put buoys where you have to go, they put them where you don't have to f***ing go. It was obvious what was going to happen – well, it was to me: another one of those Aquarius moments, which seems to be a bad omen for me. We ground to a halt; we had landed on a sandbank.

Josh started to strip down to his underpants, murmuring to himself, 'Oh well, a man's got to do what a man's got to do', as he rolled himself a rollup. As John Wayne would say. I asked him what that would be, and he said, 'Get out and push it.'

I looked at him. 'Push it? Push it? I haven't bought a f***ing boat to push it! Anyhow you've just had a heart attack, you won't be able to push it.'

He said, 'Well someone's got to', and jumped over the side.

The water was about 3 feet deep. I followed, not too keenly, but I couldn't let him push it on his own. We eventually, every time a wave came in, managed to push it a couple of yards until it was in deep water.

It was now well past midnight and there wasn't a light to be seen, and we didn't have any lights. I was now back on the bow of the boat and Josh, who was steering, kept asking me if I could see anything familiar, which I couldn't. But suddenly out of the darkness came a big round object.

'There's something coming towards us,' I said.

'What is it?' he asked.

'F****d if I know, it's big and round and there's a big chain on it,' I replied.

We just missed it; it was a large buoy which real ships would be anchored to. After going on for about a mile Josh was still asking if I recognized anywhere, which I didn't. I felt the boat gradually bearing left and thought that Josh was in more familiar territory, although I wasn't so sure. I then became aware that the tide had turned and it was running out at a terrific speed. Suddenly the boat again ground to a halt. About 100 yards in front of us was a well-lit-up area, which we found out later were grain silos. Well, we couldn't go anywhere as we were well and truly stuck in the mud and as we were all knackered; we put our heads down and got some sleep.

I was awakened by the seagulls screaming and squawking away overhead, and very severe stomach pains. I badly needed a crap. The others were still asleep, so I looked around for something to do it in. The only things I could find were an old paint tin and an old greasy rag. Being constantly dive bombed by the sea gulls, I went about my business, later to find, that I had a perfectly round black ring on my arse. The last time anything like that had happened was in the hop fields of Kent, just after the war. The only difference then was no paint tin but I had squatted my arse on some rather painful stinging nettles.

As I had finished my toilet, I looked around the boat to see if I could recognise where we were. I soon found out.

'Josh, Josh!' I shouted. 'For f**k's sake wake up, we are well in the shit.' And I didn't mean the one I had just slung over the side in the tin. 'Come outside and take a look,' I said.

He came out of the cabin, rolling his fag, and said, 'What's up?'

'That's what's f***ing up,' I said, pointing over the side of the boat.

What he saw, must have made even his wonky ticker miss a beat, for the boat had ground to a halt straddled across a fissure in the river bed, the bow resting on one side, the stern on the other. We had to wait around for the tide to come back in to refloat us again. When, at dawn, we were able to establish where we were, it became clear that we (or Josh) had steered up the River Roach, a small tributary off the River Crouch.

We made our way back to the River Crouch and upriver to the North Fambridge Yachting Station where I had arranged a berth for the boat. The boys ran to the bungalow to let Lena and Joan know that we were all well. Apparently, they had alerted all the rescue services, who were out looking for us.

Our days at the Thatched House were now coming to an end, we had been there for 13 years, and were approaching middle age. We looked at many public houses and were very taken with one, the Crown at Langdon Hills, Laindon, which was on the outskirts of Basildon, Essex. The outgoing landlord was Ronnie Hinson, one of three famous professional boxing brothers. The pub was perched on the top of a hill which had a notice board stating that it was the highest pub in the county of Essex. The pub had its own cricket ground and was set in a beautiful country park. It looked idyllic. But they all look like that, at

The Crown at Langdon Hills, Laindon.

first! It was an old coaching house and was quite a few hundred years old. In fact one of the old regulars, whose family had lived in the area for centuries, showed me a census form from those days, which read:

On the night of ....
that on that night of the census
the coaching house inhabitants consisted of
1 landlord, 1 landlord's wife, 1 serving wench,
1 coach driver, 1 groom, 2 passengers

Lena and I decided to take the Crown and prepared to move. When I told Josh where we were going to, he said, 'What, the plastic bikers' pub?' I asked him what he meant by that, he replied, that everyone called it that as the public bar was full of bikers who wore plastic bikers' outfits but none of them had any motor bikes. 'They like a bit of trouble too' he said. F***ing arseholes, out of the bleeding frying pan into the fire, I said to myself.

My brother Alec and his wife had now joined the company and had taken over a pub called the Railway, Pitsea. As he lived only about ten minutes from the pub it was ideal for Jean, as she could go home for a couple of hours a day to get away for a while: running a pub is a very stressful business.

Josh was giving me a hand with the move, while Joan was helping Lena to organise the furniture into the moving vans. Eventually they set off. Tracey led the way in his little Mini Minor with the Alsatian, Lena's two poodles and four cat baskets, each with a cat within. As was obvious, it was a recipe for disaster: one of the cats managed to escape, Sheba the Alsatian thought it was lunchtime, climbing and jumping all around the interior of the car, with the poodles giving that innocent, 'nothing to do with me' look, while the cat was shitting itself, literally. Tracey's lovely light tan car interior was now a shitty-smelling streaky dark brown, mixed with blood, as the cat had been bitten. The odour of cat shit was now fourfold as the three other cats' bowels had exploded through the bottom of the cages. Sheba, who was originally sitting in the passenger's seat, was now sitting in the back seat with the caged cats, and the poodles had scampered under the front seat, keeping the shitty cat company.

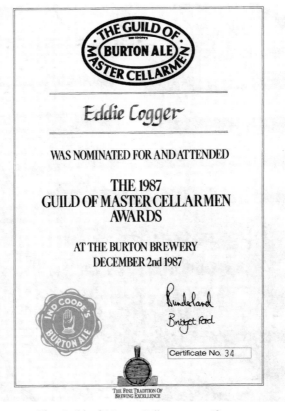

The Guild of Master Cellarmen certificate.

40

The Crown

When we opened in the evening, Josh was right: all long hair, plastic outfits, but no bikes. Contrary to Josh's opinion of them, they were no trouble at all.

We gradually began to introduce different themes to the pub. Firstly we built a children's zoo, which included three goats, 20-odd rabbits, chickens, the four cats which had become five (we were adopted by a little crippled wild cat who lived in a derelict old barn that belonged to the brewery), the Alsatian and the two poodles (who loved all the fuss they were getting), ducks, etcetera. We were very surprised one day to find the rabbits were bonking the ducks; I have never come across that before, I guess I could have been done for allowing porno animals to do what they did in front of children? Well it was 25 years ago!

Eddie was a very industrious young man. He had now passed his

Residents of the children's zoo.

City & Guilds as a cook and was working at Plaistow Hospital. He was a good worker with a pleasant personality – and he didn't pass his courses as I did, by the drunken mistake of a Cook Sergeant. But he had to travel from the Crown to Plaistow and work a ten-hour shift, and then travel back again to the Crown. It began to get too much for him so he began to look for another job. We offered him a job as the cook at the Crown, which he took until he found himself another permanent job. A regular customer at the Crown, who himself was once a landlord, ran a local company called Jubilee Windows. Eddie asked if he needed any staff and was well pleased when he was offered a job. He eventually became a double glazing window fabricator and worked for us at weekends, doing the cooking.

We then employed a cook and began to serve posh meals: no more plastic-looking ham or cheese sandwiches turned up at the edges, but real food. The serving of food had proved very successful and we were reaping the rewards. We started having live music, which was also a great success. We then introduced children's swings, slides, climbing frames, etcetera. After a couple of years the company could see the effort we had put into the pub and rewarded us by completely revamping it. The company sent us on holiday whilst the renovation was on going.

In our spare time we spent a lot of the time on the *Sea Lena* but we were nervous of going too far. We had already had an Aquarius moment the first time we took her out without Josh. Well, actually, we hadn't even taken her out yet. The scenario was like this. The yacht club at North Fambridge has moorings where you tie up and walk along the landing to the clubhouse; in the middle of the river there are river moorings; and then there are the mud bank moorings, which when the tide goes out lowers your boat onto the mud. Then, when the tide comes back in, the boat rises with the tide. Well that's the theory anyway.

But the *Sea Lena* doesn't seem to understand that she has to rise with the tide like all the other little boats, but likes to get stuck on the mud. The manager of the boatyard phoned me up one day, to tell me that the boat was stuck in the mud again and should he lift it up out of the water and refloat it again. As we lived in the village, about five minutes from the boatyard, I explained that we were expecting to go out in her that day and I would be grateful if he would. As I thought the moorings costs would cover the bill I was surprised when he presented me with one. When I queried it, he flew into one.

'F**k me, mate, what do you expect? I have had the crane down here three times now to lift your f***ing boat out of the water and you are

186

Sea Lena stuck on the mud.

complaining about the cost. If you don't like it take the bloody thing somewhere else.'

He knew he had me over a barrel (I wonder where that saying came from. Being a landlord, I wonder if it was something to do with a serving wench over a barrel, in the old days?) So I apologised to him unreservedly, as he did to me for overreacting the way he did.

So, the *Sea Lena* now afloat, I began to give Lena instructions on how to steer it, as I had to untie the ropes fore and aft to set the boat free. I showed Lena – my wife, not the boat (confusing both having the same name!) – how to switch the key to the engine on and how to put the boat into reverse, as I had to jump on as it was slowly reversing. As I jumped I slipped and, managing to hold on to the rope, was dragged into the river.

Lena, looking behind her, gently reversing into the main stream of the river where all the posh yachts and motor cruisers were moored gently bobbing up and down, hadn't realised my plight and began to panic as she headed for them. Turning round to call me she realised I wasn't on board. Screaming for me, she saw me hanging onto the side of the boat which I had just managed to reach. How on earth she managed to pull me on board I will never know.

I raced to the wheelhouse to steer the *Sea Lena* away from the posh boats, which were gradually getting closer and turned the steering wheel to stop the approaching danger. I suppose it was inevitable that two stupid pricks (especially with my experience at sea) would get the reaction we did – absolutely nothing! The f***ing thing wouldn't steer, I found the little plastic gas filled hooter Josh had taken the piss out of and pressed it to warn the boats in the middle of the river that we were out of control. Guess what, no gas, typical me.

I then found out why the boat wouldn't steer. Apparently (I was told) when the boat was rising and falling with the tides, the rudder had been forced out of the key or keep, by the boat sinking into the mud, making the boat unable to steer. We then had no alternative; I put the gear stick into forward, drove straight onto the mud again and put the bleeding thing up for sale.

I hadn't heard from my old mate Josh for some time now, he would have been most amused at our antics on the *Sea Lena*. I can imagine his reaction: 'Stupid pair of bastards', especially putting it up for sale after all the hard work he had put into repairing it.

The Crown was now in the final stages of the refit and we went back to prepare the pub for the reopening. The opening day was a big success. The company made a big show on the day by introducing a new Australian beer. The brewery had arranged for the magnificent Shire horses and dray to be in attendance and the first pint of Castlemaine XXXX was given free to each customer. There was also a 'Find the Diamond Ring Competition', which two grateful young ladies won.

The Management, Lena and I introducing the new lager – 'Castlemaine XXXX'.

The Area Manager, me and Lena welcoming The Romford Breweries' Shire horses.

Me and Marcella (our goat) welcoming the Australian cricketers and Marcella
taking exception to the kangaroo.

The Australians, who were in the country to play England in the test matches, were invited to the Crown to do the reopening ceremony and we had a fancy dress party based on an Australian theme.

The company also hired a helicopter, which landed on the cricket pitch opposite the pub. I went to meet it with my shorts on, straw hat and Marcella (the goat) attached to a lead, with a placard around her neck with 'KANGAROO' written on it. The pilot was waving at me frantically and I was waving back enthusiastically, until I realised he wanted me to get out of the f***ing way (I could see him mouthing it). Marcella didn't need telling: she had it away with me in tow, my little legs doing about 60 miles an hour.

When the helicopter had landed and the pilot had given me a right old bollocking, the doors opened and about six Aussies alighted along with a person in a kangaroo costume, which Marcella took great exception to (there's only one kangaroo here and that's me, attitude). The day was a great success and a grand day was had by all.

With 'pass the parcel' now a thing of the past, some managers were still having difficulties and still having to duck and dive to give a stock surplus, which the breweries demanded. With the renovation of the Crown and other pubs, the company had now introduced computerised tills. Each till now had every item that was for sale on the keyboard. In theory, if £1,000 of items were sold on a certain day, then £1,000 of cash should be in the till. However, theories and people don't work together: the computer doesn't tell you if a barmaid gives her fancy man free drinks, or a barman gives change for a £20 note when he's only been given a £5 note. So to keep his job the poor old manager had to resort to ducking and diving.

It is alleged that some managers had one or two trusted employees who would go to a till which was in a position where the customer couldn't see it and under-ring the item bought, but put the correct money in the till, which would make the till over. For example, sell four pints, go to the till out of sight of the customer and key in one pint but take for four pints: at the end of the day the landlord will have an excess amount of cash in the till. He would then phone a retailer (having done his own stock check) and order an amount of goods which would be needed to put the stock back in order. However, as the brewery's prices would be treble the retailer's price, a clever landlord could allegedly keep his stock in order and have no financial worries; it was like an in-lieu payment for all the bashings one took.

Our eldest son Eddie had now got married and his wife presented us

Lena's mum with first grandchild baby Angeline.

Tracey just under two years old.

Tracey aged five learning his trade for later in life.

191

with our first granddaughter, Angeline. Unfortunately Lena's mum died some months later, so my darling little Lena was now an orphan. Even though she was in her fifties, she was still a child in my eyes.

Meanwhile Tracey was working in the printing department of McAlpines, the construction firm. As you can see from the photos taken with me when he was just a nipper, he was fearless. He has a very bubbly personality and used to do a bit of ducking and diving on the job (selling cheap towels and other bits and pieces he could get hold of). He, like his mother, has a very Cockney accent – well, I suppose we all have!

One day, whilst he was at work, he was waiting for the lift to come down. A person, who he described as a very posh bloke, was also waiting for the lift to come down. As they both got into the lift, Tracey said to him, 'Oi, mate, do you want to buy any towels?' The man asked how much they were. Tracey named the price he wanted and the man tried to bait him down but Tracey wouldn't lower the price. The man bought some cheap towels off Tracey. It turned out that the man was Lord McAlpine!

41

Training Manager

About 1985 I was asked if Lena and I would like to become training managers. We jumped at the chance as it would mean an extra pair of hands to help us. It worked out well for us as it would give us some time to enjoy a rest at the bungalow.

One day, I was having a week's break down at the bungalow and Lena and I were going for lunch at the village pub, the Ferry Boat Inn. As I was approaching the bar, I heard a voice behind me say jokingly, 'Hello Ed, you too stuck up to talk to us now?' Looking over my shoulder I saw Roger Attewell, the friend we had dropped off at Tilbury on the day we made the disastrous boat journey on the road to perdition. I hadn't seen him for about three years and it was so good to see a friendly face again. However, he was bringing some devastating news, Josh had had a fatal heart attack.

I recalled the day we launched the boat and his glib and unassuming manner when he had said, 'Well, we will just have to push it then', whilst rolling a roll-up. And me screaming at him, 'Push it? F***ing, push it? I never bought a boat to push it!' I just hope that push (he had a dickey heart) wasn't the beginning of the end for him. Still, Josh was his own man and if he had made his mind up no one could change it. It was lovely knowing him, he was a man's man. He was a lovely friend. God bless you Josh.

On Christmas Day 1992 my dear old dad died of a heart attack. We had had our problems over the years but he had mellowed in his later years and, after all, I was only a chip off the same block. My darling mum died in December 1999; she was then living in a private nursing home as she was a diabetic and had to have daily care, which we were not able to administer. God bless you both.

42

The Beginning of the End

We were now coming to the end of our management career, not by design but by accident (not another one?). We were still training future publicans for the company. One couple I particularly remember. I can recall the man very well, as he lived not far from me when I was a young lad. I suppose he was about eight years older than me. I recall a bomb dropping adjacent to his house, killing two children who were in my class. His name was Bill Noyce and his wife was Vi. He became a councillor, and then later Mayor of Dagenham. All the local licensees used to take drinks to the Mayor's Chambers about four times a year and a good booze-up was had by all. He also ran a security firm, from which I bought one of his Alsatian pups. When we moved to Heath Park Estate in the sweep's van, our near neighbours were Bill and Vi and their two daughters, who were friends of our two sons.

After he had served his term as Mayor, he applied to the brewery for a manager's position and was accepted as a trainee manager. I recall that Bill had been fast-tracked as a trainee, as the brewery felt it would benefit from having a high-profile person in their employ. In fact I had some input to his training, as I had to teach him the skills he would need in his cellar techniques.

The public house that Bill and Vi had been selected to manage was the Elm Park Hotel, which was one of the first to have a bar with a separate name: this was named the Carousel Bar. My own pub had a similar set-up with a bar called Reflections, and that's when the music groups began to become popular in the pubs.

Our second granddaughter Krystle was born prematurely and was very ill during her early years. So we set up a charity to donate to the Premature Baby Unit at Basildon Hospital and another for a Children's Special Needs School called Elmbrook School, Basildon. We also collected for the British Heart Foundation and the photo below shows one of our organised charity runs from the Crown Pub. Krystle is now mother to our lovely little great-grandson, Bradley.

Charity run from The Crown.

43

Prince Charlie

My sister-in-law, Jean, was spending a few hours at home doing some housework whilst my brother was running his pub. She heard a commotion outside her house so she opened her front door. To her astonishment Prince Charles, who had just opened a home for pensioners opposite her house, was standing there.

As you know, you are not allowed to touch a royal but Jean, with a Dick Emery touch on his arm, asked him if he would like a cup of tea, to which he replied, 'No, thank you.'

Still touching his arm she said, 'Oh you are naughty, but I do like you, Charlie.' And, as you can see in the photo, they both laughed their heads off!

Jean and Prince Charles.

44

The Final Countdown

During our years of hard work for the brewery we were good and loyal employees, and we worked for them through some extremely difficult times. There was my lovely Lena's alcoholism and nervous breakdowns, the difficult lives my two sons had to endure whilst we trained and during the following years in the pubs, often physically abused by schoolmates whose parents had had a problem with us in the pubs, and were taking it out on our boys. But they grew into hard little bastards and managed to cope with anything that came their way.

I myself had to have an operation to have my prostate gland removed. Later in life I suffered a brain bleed (all the punches I had taken to the head, no doubt), then a stroke, then angina, so the management of pubs had taken a toll on all the family.

So, back to my accident. The introduction of new technology into the brewing industry caused many problems with retraining managers in computer knowledge. Apart from the computer tills, the actual computers were mainly put in some very odd places: storerooms, cupboards, etcetera. Mine was put in the only place they could find, in the tiny pantry that doubled as my office. The heavy computer was placed on a very flimsy shelf which, this being a very old pub, was only appropriate for what it was intended for: four candles or fork handles as the Two Ronnies would say. The shelf seemed to be quite flimsy to me, not having been a carpenter (office boy, yes; bookie's runner, yes; sailor, yes; soldier, yes; bookie, yes; publican, yes; but carpenter, no). The weight the flimsy shelf had to carry caused it to start giving way and, despite my continuous phone calls to the brewery, nothing was done. The inevitable happened: the shelf collapsed, pinning me under the computer, causing serious damage to my spine.

I was off sick for many months, encased in a plaster cast again. Luckily for me it was a different hospital to the one where the poofter plasterer had delicately and lovingly smoothed the plaster of Paris just inches from my Old Bill, all those years ago, but the embarrassment was just the same. Some time later I was still suffering from severe spinal pains and was declared disabled. I had to leave the brewery after serving 25 years with them, at the age of 55. As I had another ten years to go before I would my get old age pension, I was in Shit Street.

I took legal advice and was advised to sue the company for criminal negligence, as I had repeatedly warned the company of the dangerous state that the shelf was in. The company admitted that I had repeatedly warned them and made an offer of £35,000 pounds, which on the advice of my lawyers, I refused. They argued that I had lost an income of £20,000 a year, and then there was the pain and suffering I had endured and would endure for the rest of my life, and that the offer was inadequate. They came back with another offer of £50,000, and again I refused.

When the court broke for lunch, I heard two of the other side's lawyers talking to each other saying, 'But his injuries were caused when he was a steel erector.' I was well choked when I realised I had turned down £50,000, but there wasn't anything I could do about it now; the court was being called back in to hear the Judge's verdict.

Our retirement party in 1989. I was 55 years old, Lena was 52.

My heart sank when the Judge said he hadn't had much to decide on, in coming to a decision on this case. I looked over at the two opposition lawyers, smirking all over their faces. 'I find in favour of...' – come on, put me out of my misery – 'the plaintiff, Mr E.L. Cogger. As the brewery has admitted liability and Mr Cogger has now an uncertain future in front of him, I have taken into consideration that Mr Cogger who was a longstanding senior manager with the brewery should be awarded the sum of ...' – wait for it – 'one hundred and forty thousand pounds.' Cop hold of that one Ed, me boy!

45

The Apartment in Cyprus

We decided to spend some of the money we had worked for, and literally shed blood and tears for in the company over the last 25 years, on a lovely two-bed apartment in Cyprus. I had banked the £140,000 that the court had awarded me, despite the assertions of the two opposition lawyers that I had pulled the wool over the Judge's eyes, not only in this case but also in the previous case when I was awarded nearly £10,000. How could I, a moderately educated person have had the brains to beat the legal system like that! Let me tell you (as one Northern comic used to say), the only one who got any pleasure out of my injuries that day was the bent plasterer of Paris who lovingly strung me up, with my dingle-dangle at eye level, and gently plastered me from the chest down.

Melania Gardens, Block 5, apartments and swimming pool.

About 30 years previously Lena had gone to the local fish and chip shop where she saw a beautiful pure white cat with four equally white kittens. The mother and the four kittens all had one pure blue eye and one amber eye. Lena fell in love with them and asked if she could buy one, and the owner agreed to let her buy one when it was old enough to leave its mother. By coincidence the fish shop was called Costers, probably the most popular name in Cyprus.

Lena called the kitten Shona, the same as the mother. 'Shona' means 'pure white' in Greek. Unfortunately, when we were training and had been working away to do a holiday relief (the boys were with their grandparents), Shona, who was about a year old, was found dead by Lena. She had died either of heartbreak or poisoning.

However, back to Cyprus in 2007 and Coincidence Number Two. I normally, every morning, went for a walk but the sun was very hot that morning, so Lena and I just sat in the shade on our balcony. Suddenly Lena let out a cry: 'Shona, it's Shona!'

I looked at her, wondering what she was going on about, she was staring behind me. Looking around I saw a beautiful pure white cat with one blue eye and one amber eye. She walked straight into the living room and jumped up on my lap and started rubbing her head all over me, as if she known me all her life. She stayed with us in the apartment for the next six weeks of our holiday, and followed me on my daily walk around the area without ever leaving me.

Shona.

As the time to go home came, we worried what we would do with her, so I decided to build her a little kennel on the balcony. We also bought the largest cat feeder, which we filled up with dry cat food, and hoped she would survive for a while, at least. We knew this was somewhat futile as Cyprus has a huge population of stray cats and kittens, thousands and thousands of them, many of them becoming road victims. On the day of our return home, we tearfully said goodbye to Shona. We knew we wouldn't see her again as we wouldn't be back for another three months.

After three months at home, we again returned to Cyprus. It was nearing midnight as the taxi drove into the complex and we wearily unloaded our luggage and quickly retired to bed. In the morning I drew back the curtains to a glorious sunny day, and I looked up, surveying the beautiful picturesque scenery and mountains stretching as far as the eye could see, sweeping down to the beautiful blue sea of the Mediterranean.

I looked down to see the little box that I had made for Shona empty. With a heavy heart and tears running down my cheeks, I saw that the dry food container was also empty. At least we had done our best for her. After breakfast, whilst Lena sunbathed at the pool, I took my normal walk around the complex. I reached a particular scenic area, a valley which looked like a garden centre run wild with flowers, shrubs, trees, cactuses, etcetera, an impenetrable mass of colour. It was a wonderful view. As I began to move away, I heard a sound like a baby crying, which I thought most unusual. I carried on with my walk, but I heard it again. Turning around I saw Shona running towards me, calling me. If you believe in miracles read on.

Lena couldn't believe her eyes when she saw Shona. 'Where did you find her?' she asked.

'She found me,' I replied, explaining what had happened.

'I can't believe it,' she said, 'it's a miracle.'

Shona was an amazing cat, almost human. Lena and I discussed what we should do with her, as we would be returning back home soon. We decided that we would keep her for another week. In the meantime we went to a vet to see if they would put an advert in their window to help us find her a home, which they agreed to. We put my mobile phone number on the advert. We carried on with the remaining days of our holiday, and Shona used to pop in and out of the French windows or lie on the balcony when we went out, or to the beach.

On this particular day we were on the beach and my mobile began to ring, which was most unusual as I rarely carried it with me. Coincidence

Number Three. It was the vet, who said that a woman had brought in a pure white cat to be put down and it resembled the cat we had sought a good home for – could we come down and identify it. We did, and it was Shona. We knew the woman who took her in, but she obviously wasn't a cat lover as we were.

We asked the vet what we could do and she said that there was only one solution: take away her babies and have her spayed. I explained that we had to go home in a couple of days and we wouldn't be back for three months, so there wouldn't be anyone to care for her. We didn't know what to do, so we made a decision which we knew in our hearts was the right one, we decided to bring her back to England.

She had her babies removed, she was spayed, and had to spend six months in quarantine. She was very ill for some time, but gradually recovered. This was to be our final trip to Cyprus; we had noticed that property values were reaching their peak and were beginning to fall, and we put the apartment up for sale. We went to see Shona before she was due to fly to England. She looked absolutely beautiful in her little one up one down house in the cattery. Although there were hundreds of strays in the grounds of the cattery, they all got a meal too.

Well, as we had another cat at home, Dina, we wondered how she would take to this youngster in the white coat. We went to Heathrow to pick up Shona, and as we put her on the seat in her little box her eyes (one blue one amber) looked straight into mine and she meowed and it sounded just like 'Hello'. She was well worth the £2,600 she had cost in six months of treatment, six months' kennelling, and the flight from Cyprus and quarantine costs. She has certainly lifted the hearts of two grateful people.

Lena and I, with the two boys, celebrated that night with a visit to our lovely little village pub, the Ferry Boat Inn. Due to the court case, I hadn't visited the pub for some time but I had learned that a new tenant had been found to take the pub.

We walked into the bar, ordered our drinks and a voice from the past bellowed out in a typically landlord's manner, 'Who let that expert on fiddling claims into my pub? He will trip over the doorstep and sue me next, the fiddling bastard.'

Looking round to where the voice came from, I could hardly believe who I saw: a person I had known basically all my life, Bill Noyce. As I looked at him, it seemed that his life flashed in front of my eyes. The schoolboy who went to the seniors while I was in the juniors; the young man who walked past our house, whilst I swung on the broken garden gate, coming home from his work at Prichard & Gold; his meteoric rise as a very young man to shop steward; his election as Mayor of Dagenham, his successful security business (from which we bought our lovely Alsatian Sheba); his success when changing direction and going into management in the licensing trade; then his venture into the restaurant business at Elm Park; and finally taking over the Ferry Boat Inn as mine host.

All these positions were taken with his lovely wife Vi at his side. Unfortunately Bill passed away some years ago. Vi is now in a home; she is fragile but always keeps smiling and still visits the pub frequently, which is now run by her daughter Sylvia, who sadly lost her husband Roy a few years ago.

THE FERRY BOAT INN

North Fambridge, Essex CM3 6LR

The 500 year old riverside pub now offers accommodation as well as its renowned food, beers and hospitality.
SEE INSIDE FOR DETAILS
or ring
01621 740208

The Ferry Boat Inn.

Tracey as 'Sean Curtis'.

46

The End

Well, that's it, the end of my experiences through my life. I am now 75 years young, my beautiful little Lena is now 72 years young and our two sons Eddie and Tracey are old, very old. (No, I am only joking.)

Both of my boys are talented in their own way. Tracey went into singing and slapstick comedy and ended up doing television, appearing in *EastEnders* and *The Bill.* He has a lovely voice and ever since he was a little boy, he has been very talented. I sincerely apologise to Eddie and Tracey for all the stress that I put them through, but looking back, what could I do? I was unemployable in my previous trades due to earlier injuries. I ducked and dived my way through life and was clever enough to create a situation that benefited us all. I regret all the pain that I have put them through mentally, but there were the trappings of

Above: Amelia (Tina's daughter).

Left: Ellis and Amber, with parents Tracey and Tracey

Eddie and his daughters, Krystle, Gabrielle, Jade and Angeline.

My mum and dad celebrating their 50th wedding anniversary. I was then 52 years old and Lena 49 years old.

Bradley, son of Krystle Cogger and Lennie, son of Angeline Cogger.

Me aged 70 years old.

success as well: buying the bungalow, buying a holiday home in Cyprus, holidays every year, racehorses, greyhounds, cruises. Their mother and I love them both dearly. God bless them both and their families.

My younger son Tracey married a girl called Tracey (see, I told you we were strange) and gave us a beautiful granddaughter called Amber, and a grandson called Ellis. My eldest son Eddie has four girls: Angeline, Krystle, Jade and Gabrielle.

Unfortunately Eddie's wife, having had four quick pregnancies, couldn't cope with the situation and, when the girls had reached their early teens she left Eddie and the girls and went her own way to start a new life. When she left, Eddie had to give up his job to look after the girls, who were still at school.

Angel and Krystle have recently presented us with two wonderful great-grandsons, so my lovely little Lena's and my own circle of life is now complete. Or is it?